Rearing children in our contemporary culture is difficult, but rearing grateful children is even harder. In *Raising Grateful Kids in an Entitled World*, Kristen Welch gives solid practical advice. Grateful children become responsible adults. I highly recommend this book.

GARY CHAPMAN, PH.D.
Author of *The Five Love Languages*

In this fast-paced, instant gratification culture, Kristen's countercultural message of selflessness and gratitude is much needed! This book left me convicted, challenged, and encouraged, both personally and as a parent.

CRYSTAL PAINE
Founder of MoneySavingMom.com and *New York Times* bestselling author of *Say Goodbye to Survival Mode*

I absolutely love this book. Kristen unearths the heart issue of why many children are selfish and unaware of the needs of others. Her words engage, inspire, and instruct parents in raising emotionally strong, healthy children who are grateful in the important moments of life.

SALLY CLARKSON
Author of *The Lifegiving Home* and *Own Your Life*, and blogger at SallyClarkson.com

Kristen's words are so timely, and I am thankful for her hard-fought wisdom. I am all ears whenever Kristen writes because she just gets it, and it was no different with this book. If you're looking for support and practical ideas on how to raise grateful kids in an increasingly entitled world, this book is a must-read.

SARAH MAE
Author of *Longing for Paris*

I can't think of anyone I would trust more than Kristen to teach on this topic. She's made her entire life a testimony to doing this well, and everyone who reads this book will be inspired by her story, her heart, her wisdom, and her love of the Lord.

ANGIE SMITH
Bestselling author of several books and Bible studies including *Chasing God* and *Seamless*

Parents today fight what seems like a never-ending battle against the current of the culture in raising our children. In *Raising Grateful Kids in an Entitled World*, Kristen not only inspires us to raise our children differently, but she teaches us how to actually live that out in our homes. So very practical and convicting. A must-read!

RUTH SCHWENK
Pastor's wife and mama to four, coauthor of *Hoodwinked*, and creator of TheBetterMom.com

RAISING GRATEFUL KIDS IN AN ENTITLED WORLD

RAISING

GRATEFUL
KIDS
IN AN
ENTITLED
WORLD

HOW ONE FAMILY LEARNED THAT SAYING NO
CAN LEAD TO LIFE'S BIGGEST YES

KRISTEN WELCH

**TYNDALE®
MOMENTUM**

AN IMPRINT OF TYNDALE HOUSE PUBLISHERS, INC.

Visit Tyndale online at www.tyndale.com.

Visit Tyndale Momentum online at www.tyndalemomentum.com.

Tyndale Momentum and the Tyndale Momentum logo are registered trademarks of Tyndale House Publishers, Inc. Tyndale Momentum is an imprint of Tyndale House Publishers, Inc., Carol Stream, Illinois 60188.

Raising Grateful Kids in an Entitled World: How One Family Learned That Saying No Can Lead to Life's Biggest Yes

Designed by Ron Kaufmann

Edited by Bonne Steffen

Published in association with the literary agency of William K. Jensen Literary Agency, 119 Bampton Court, Eugene, OR 97404.

Library of Congress Cataloging-in-Publication Data

Welch, Kristen.
    Raising grateful kids in an entitled world : how one family learned that saying no can lead to life's biggest yes / Kristen Welch.
        pages cm
    Includes bibliographical references.
    ISBN 978-1-4964-0529-6 (sc)
    1. Child rearing—Religious aspects—Christianity. 2. Parenting—Religious aspects—Christianity. 3. Gratitude—Religious aspects—Christianity. I. Title.
    BV4529.W45 2015
    248.8'45—dc23   2015030200

Printed in the United States of America

21   20   19   18   17   16
7   6   5   4   3

For my family
and every other family who dares to live upstream

CONTENTS

INTRODUCTION

A FORD F-150 PICKUP TRUCK sits in our driveway. My husband, Terrell, wears a cowboy hat on Saturday to mow the lawn and his western boots every day of the week. We grow our own tomatoes and fry okra every chance we get, and we are the proud owners of our very own septic system.

It's not uncommon to park behind a horse trailer at the Target or Chick-fil-A down the street from our house. We aren't really country; we are just Texans, and proud of it. We love our big green backyard, the friendly neighbors, and the slower pace. And cowboy boots are a part of our story.

Every spring we go to the Houston Livestock Show and Rodeo. It's not only a big deal around these parts; it's the biggest indoor rodeo in the United States. We set aside money for this annual outing for our family to cover our meals, tickets for the events, and an extra-special fried treat.

A couple of years ago, we decided it was high time our three growing kids got their first pair of cowboy boots. You might call it a rite of passage for children in Texas and the western states. We budgeted even more than usual, setting our sights to purchase them at the rodeo because we knew there would be plenty to choose from as well as special deals that would save us money.

On the hour trip downtown, one of my kids (who will remain nameless) complained about the seat arrangements in the van, the heat, and the very air siblings dared to breathe. I corrected said child, and I was half tempted to squash the dream of boots, leaving this one scuffling along in tennis shoes, but after a quick apology was received, grace won out.

We headed straight to the Justin Boots booth and helped all three of our kids try on and choose boots that (1) they loved and (2) we could afford—which was a feat in and of itself because my kids can be picky and boots are expensive. But we accomplished our goal in under an hour and spent the rest of the day in new boots—looking at animals, watching roping events, and eating large amounts of food that probably shouldn't be fried. (I'm looking at you, bacon and Oreos.)

On the way home, the same child's bad attitude surfaced again, this time about not getting to do something at the rodeo. It wasn't just whining, the result of a tiring day; it was ingratitude and entitlement. Complaints and warnings fired in rapid succession between the backseat and the front. The day had been a splurge from the beginning, but it wasn't appreciated. But mostly, it wasn't enough. Even after grace put a nice pair of boots on the kid's feet.

Halfway home, in the middle of the tense ride with an unrepentant boot wearer in the backseat, Terrell said, "That's it. When we get home, I want you to pack your boots back in the box. I'll see if we can't return them to Cavender's [a local boot store]."

This nearly broke my Texas heart, but I knew it was the right thing to do.

We didn't buy the boots to take them away. As a matter of fact, at first Terrell couldn't find the receipt after he said it. As he fumbled in his pocket, I bit my lip because this parenting thing is so hard. We wanted our child to enjoy our generous gift for the feet, but it was the heart that needed immediate attention.

It saddened me to hear the tears, the begging, the promises. Then the question, "Why can't you show me grace?"

"Buying you the boots in the first place *was* grace," I said.

Once we were home, Terrell put the boxed boots on a high shelf in the laundry room and said, "If you want the boots, you'll have to work for them." He pointed to the huge mulched areas in the front and back yards. "You have three days to pull every weed. I won't remind you; it's up to you. This job will pay for your boots. This time you're going to earn them."

And that was that.

The rodeo happens in early March, usually before we have a chance to clean up winter's effect on our yard. My gaze followed my husband's pointing finger to the weedy mulch beds, and my heart sank. It was going to be a lot of work. Lo, the weeds were many.

My husband is hardly a dictator. He's kind and loving and a lot nicer than I am most days. But I could tell by the firmness in his voice and the tilt of his chin that he was serious. *This* was serious. The mounting ingratitude that had been an issue for weeks had to be addressed. I wanted to high-five him and sob at the same time.

I wondered what our child would choose.

My heart soared a little while later when I heard the front door click. I looked out the window and saw my kid wearing old clothes, bent down in the wet mulch. It had started to rain.

For the next two days, I watched from that window. A little proud, a little brokenhearted, but with every pulled weed, I knew the hard work was making for a softer heart.

When Terrell handed back the boots after hearing a meaningful apology, I knew we had all won. "You earned these," he said. "I won't take them away again."

The boots meant twice as much.

It will go down in our family history as the infamous boot story. It was the day we generously bought our kids cowboy boots. It was the same day we took them away because of ingratitude. It definitely wasn't the first day my kids acted unthankful—and there have been many times since.

With every pulled weed, I knew the hard work was making for a softer heart.

But it was a day we called out entitlement in our home and waged war against it. It was the day we reestablished the fact that we wanted to raise grateful kids more than anything else.

If you ask most parents what they want for their kids, they say, "I want them to be happy." Most might even have the same answer for themselves. Instead of happiness being a by-product of the life we live, it has become an elusive destination. And our culture is obsessed with pursuing it. We go into debt for it. We leave our marriages to attain it. We allow child-centered homes in hopes that our kids can achieve it. That's not to say we aren't doing a great job in some areas.

I agree with Dan Kindlon, a psychiatrist and author of *Too Much of a Good Thing*:

> Compared to earlier generations, we are emotionally closer to our kids, they confide in us more, we have more fun with them, and we know about the science of child development. But we are too indulgent. We give our kids too much and demand too little of them.[1]

Let me say that I've always been close to my parents and confided in them (even to this day), but I was guilty as a young mother of often giving in to the temptation to provide fun for my kids all the time. It didn't take me long, though, to realize that too many fun days make the boring ones harder to bear.

Kindlon goes on to say,

> I find myself at the center of this problem as I try, with my wife, to balance the two major tasks of parenting: showing our kids that we love them and raising them with the skills and values they'll need to be emotionally healthy adults, which often requires that we act in ways that can anger and upset them.[2]

The bottom line, Kindlon concludes, is that parents are raising spoiled kids. I know exactly what he is talking about. When we try to protect our kids from unhappiness, we make life down the road harder for them. It can be summed up in one word—*entitlement*.

Entitlement is a hot topic today. The root word *entitled* means exactly what it says—to give someone a title or a right. It used to be reserved for the wealthy and the privileged, based upon economics or status, but now it seems to have shifted to human nature and our rights—the "feeling or belief that you deserve to be given something."[3] We live in a culture that is obsessed with the right to have what we want, whether we've earned it or not.

We live in a culture that is obsessed with the right to have what we want.

Guess what happens when you decide to deal with entitlement in your home (or dare to write a book about it)? You become your own case study. The minute we named it for what it was and began addressing it, we began to recognize it at every turn. And honestly, parenting got harder.

But at the same time, we got better at identifying it and braver at dealing with it and more dependent on God in eradicating it. We looked for ways to change perspectives, sought opportunities to serve, required hard work, and made gratitude our goal. All of these actions were evidence of our commitment to life's biggest yes—to love God and love others more than ourselves. And honestly, parenting got a little easier.

I never wanted to write a parenting book. When I started writing on my blog about gratitude in the face of entitlement, I was writing from a place of struggle, not success. I'm mother to an elementary-aged child (Emerson), a junior higher (Jon-Avery), and a high schooler (Madison). I'm writing from the middle of my mess, not from my accomplishment. I am in the thick of it. I don't have a psychology degree or a master's in counseling. I'm not an expert or a professional. I'm a mom. I'm your peer, and I'm in the trenches with you.

Terrell and I aren't perfect parents, and we make mistakes all the time. I tend to be a control freak, and I talk before I listen. I also have a temper and can be high strung (to name a few of my flaws). Terrell is more patient, but he's also a "get over it" kind of parent, and he doesn't always get our emotional daughters.

I want to tell you what this book is not—it's not a guide, nor a list of dos and don'ts. It won't offer you a fail-proof parenting plan, and it's not a guilt trip. It's not the answers to all your late-night burning questions that beg to be answered: *Does my child need more grace or more discipline right now? Am I handling this situation correctly?*

While I do bring in expert opinions and share research and some suggestions, this book is my confessional. It's a record of our journey of attempting to raise grateful kids instead of entitled ones. It's the ups and downs, the defeats and victories of such a difficult task. It's my unfinished story. It's also a history lesson from the past, a cultural lesson for the present, and a daunting challenge to learn from one and overcome the second. But mostly, this book is an encouragement to parents swimming upstream in a society that demands we do what is culturally accepted.

We are Christians, yes, and we love Jesus and we do our best to live for him. Every family is different—maybe you love God but your lives look different than ours; maybe you haven't thought much about spiritual things but would like that to change. This book is about our family's journey, and while what you'll read here is Christ-centered, you are welcome to join the journey no matter where you are coming from.

A word of caution and a disclaimer.

Anytime we step out of the mainstream and try to turn our lives (or homes) around and dare to go upstream, it's hard. Some would say impossible. The journey is filled with obstacles, naysayers, and discouragers. And then there are the children. Starting from preschool, our kids are taught conformity—to be like everyone else, to follow rules and not misstep. It's in our human makeup to want to fit in, to not stick out or be different, to blend in.

It's in our human makeup to want to fit in, to not be different.

The problem is, we are called to exactly that—to go against the flow. In one of my favorite Scriptures, followers of Jesus are encouraged to live differently than the world, to live upstream.

> Don't become so well-adjusted to your culture
> that you fit into it without even thinking. Instead,
> fix your attention on God.
> ROMANS 12:2, MSG

Not only is this way of life possible, it's commanded. But we cannot do it alone. We need God's help; we need each other's help. Because when we dare to lead in a go-against-the-flow, countercultural home, we are standing against what is accepted and "normal." We will face opposition from the world, from our children, and possibly from other Christians. It's not popular, but most good things aren't.

I'm a parent, and I wrote this book *for* parents. It's not instruction for kids or a tell-all of my children's mistakes (my intention is to share the lessons learned from my perspective, not theirs). No matter how old your kids are, you can apply the simple suggestions in leading your family upstream. At the end of every chapter, there is a section called "Going against the Flow" that contains practical, age-appropriate suggestions for grateful, countercultural living for you and your kids.

Are you ready to jump in?

Kristen Welch

PART I

LAUNCH

What separates privilege from entitlement is gratitude.

BRENÉ BROWN

CHAPTER 1

WANTS VS. NEEDS

IN ONE OF COMEDIAN Jim Gaffigan's stand-up routines, he describes how we act when we first arrive at a hotel. We walk into the lobby and exclaim, "Wow, this place is amazing!" We find our room, take a good look around, and we love it. By day two, with unmade beds and suitcases strewn across the floor, the mystique begins to wear off. Suddenly, we look around and say, "This place is a dump." When we return from a day of fun and the housekeeping staff hasn't had a chance to clean up *our* mess, we are outraged. "There's a wet towel still on the bathroom floor! How could they? I'm calling to complain!"

Gaffigan's audience explodes with laughter because it's funny. But the problem is, it's also true—and maybe that's not so funny, especially when our kids are standing next to us in the hotel room, listening to our indignant attitude. It's startling how quickly our gratitude turns into ingratitude.

But, we reason, if we've paid our hard-earned money, shouldn't we be guaranteed a good night's stay with impeccable service? We are entitled to at least that. They owe us, right?

If we look closer, we can see that this same attitude pervades not only our culture, but also our homes. We often buy things not so much because we need them, but because we feel like we deserve them. We work hard; we owe it to ourselves. It's so easy to get wrapped up in this way of thinking.

I'm guilty too.

We've been in our current home for two years. I've grown tired of the builder's drab beige walls, and I started toying with the idea of painting. But with neck and back issues of my own and a husband who loathes painting projects, I knew the only way to get it done was to hire someone. Terrell agreed it would be a great improvement, but he suggested we should wait since he was transitioning out of his corporate job into the role of CEO of our small nonprofit. He was being cautious about our finances.

I was immediately indignant. *Wait? I have waited.* And then I began to go down the list of my self-sacrifice and service, the reasons I deserved this home makeover. Terrell smiled and said, "You sort of sound entitled right now." Oh. That comment took the wind out of my sails. And honestly, it hurt my feelings because he was right.

We don't want to wait. Here in the United States, we live in a fast-paced, convenience-driven, impatient culture. Some might even say this is the beauty of the American Dream—working hard so you get what you want in life, which has attracted countless immigrants to come here. And we are very, very good at it.

THE GOOD LIFE

The term "American Dream" was first used by James Truslow Adams in 1931 in his book *The Epic of America*. There he described it as "a dream of social order in which each man and each woman shall be able to attain to the fullest stature of which they are innately capable."[1]

But I've discovered that like many things in life, definitions change. A more current description of the American Dream is "an American social ideal that stresses egalitarianism and especially material prosperity."[2] I asked my blog readers for their own perspective on the term and got dozens of responses, such as this one from Kim Frey:

> Our grandparents probably viewed it as the ability to get out of poverty, to provide for loved ones, and to have a comfortable home, getting a strong basic education, having a good work ethic, and being content with what you have. . . . I think the idea of the American Dream has become much more materialistic in the past few decades . . . "Bigger, better, faster, and more" has defined it recently.

Reader Angela Sellman agreed and added this:

> [The American Dream is] bigger, more. Newer is
> better. *Everyone* must have the newest gadget, cars,
> and *fun fun fun* at all times. Happiness all the time is
> the goal for everyone!

Or there's the definition Terrell heard on the radio years
ago that he's never forgotten:

> The American Dream is getting all you can. Canning
> all you can get. Sitting on the can so nobody can get
> what you can.

Has the dream changed? It seems to have morphed from
a rags-to-riches, hard work ethic mentality to prosperity now.
Or perhaps the dream is the same, but *we* have changed. I'm
not sure the concept can be quantified, especially considering
inflation, but I think we can all agree something has changed.
The median income of Americans has dropped considerably
since the beginning of the 2008 recession, but we're paying
over 15 percent more for new cars.

And it's not just what we drive; houses have nearly tripled
in size and families have gotten smaller. In 1950, the average
house was 983 square feet, but by 2014 it had reached 2,598
square feet.[3]

And growth like this isn't cheap. *USA Today* published a
report in 2014 that put a price tag on the American Dream:
$130,000 a year, which includes a nice six-figure salary, lux-
ury vacations, college savings, and retirement.[4]

Our family signed up for that track when my husband landed his first corporate job, after nearly ten years in full-time ministry. We finally had a 401(k), dental insurance, and a ladder to climb up. We scraped our money together, packed up our rented 1,000-square-foot townhome, and couldn't believe the sellers had accepted our bottom-dollar offer on our dream house. We moved in mid-December and scrambled to put up a Charlie Brown Christmas tree, mostly for our two kids, who were two and four years old at the time. There were a few gifts scattered underneath the tree, but we all knew we'd really gotten a house for Christmas.

But within two years of living the dream in a house I loved at first sight, I began to see it in a completely different light. And the light glared brighter every time I visited someone else's house. Why hadn't I noticed how small our living room was or how badly the floors needed work? Over time, we began to update our home. We pulled down wallpaper, hired a painter, built a sprawling deck, added a couple of walls . . . all great improvements and not bad in and of themselves. But somewhere along the way, I began referring to this house I had once dreamed of owning as our "starter home." What had once been more than enough eventually became not enough.

What had once been more than enough eventually became not enough.

Every year Christmas got bigger and bigger in that house. We put up the biggest tree we could find in the front bay window and the thousand white lights that adorned it could be seen from the street. I spent a lot of time and money decorating nearly every room. I'll never forget the Christmas morning when my kids were six and four years old and there were piles of presents under the tree, dozens for each of them. I didn't feel it was excessive because I was an organized deal shopper and had gotten most of the toys on sale months before. I was as excited as my kids, and I couldn't wait to see their faces as they opened each gift in delight.

But it didn't really happen that way. It was a blur of grabbing and tearing into gifts, and within minutes the room looked like a tornado had ripped through it. I watched my kids go from one gift to another, hardly taking the time to even remove all the paper. With piles of opened gifts and still more to go, they actually seemed tired from the exertion of opening so many. We took a break and cleaned up for a bit before we started round two. There were some gasps of delight here and there, but with a room full of stuff, I don't think I've ever felt emptier.

I pushed the depressing thought away and encouraged my kids to say thank you. To my husband, I justified the piles of presents proudly, saying it was a debt-free Christmas. But the nagging feeling stayed with me the rest of the day. I realized what bothered me that morning wasn't just about having more stuff; it was about getting more stuff. And it was my problem, as much as my kids'. Maybe more.

AN ATTITUDE IS BORN

I married my husband two weeks before Christmas in 1994. After a week honeymooning, we woke up on Christmas morning in our first apartment with dozens of wedding gifts to unwrap. It was just as romantic as it sounds. After a leisurely morning of opening presents we didn't pay for, we drove an hour to my parents' house to a feast we didn't have to prepare. We were the newlyweds, and we were special. By the next Christmas and our first anniversary, we lived hundreds of miles from home and it was my in-laws' turn to have us as Christmas guests.

I pitched a fit to my husband about it. I had never spent the holidays away from my family, and even though my husband missed his family as much as I missed mine, I acted like a spoiled brat. I whined and cried and finally gave in. We didn't have a lot of money, but I couldn't imagine not opening gifts on Christmas, so we saved $100 to spend on each other. I shopped and searched and I bought Terrell five gifts with the money.

On Christmas morning at his parents' house, the extended family opened their gifts to each other, but I didn't see any for me from my young husband. Meanwhile, he was opening his fourth one from me . . . a used Rook game off eBay. (It seemed like a good idea at the time.)

The gifts were all opened and Terrell gave me a sly look. I was trying not to cry. He went over to the tree and pulled off a papier-mâché ornament. He opened the ball to reveal a beautiful pearl necklace inside. When he put it around my neck, I said thank you—and then I went to the bathroom and cried. I was so disappointed that I only had one gift from him under the tree.

Oh, boy. I had a lot to learn. I didn't just want something; I wanted more. And when I became a mom, this attitude spilled over into my early parenting. I wanted my kids to have more, the best. I wanted them to have it all, too.

My buy-in to the notion that I needed more of the best for myself and my kids didn't satisfy me. Its pursuit actually left me feeling emptier than when I had less. Things didn't begin to shift for me until a couple of years later, when I traveled to Kenya, Africa, with Compassion International as a blogger. It was there in one of the world's largest and poorest slums that I began to see my life and my own entitlement in light of how the rest of the world lived. It shook me to the core and flipped a switch inside me that made me stop and reevaluate what was happening.

Entitlement didn't start with my kids. It began with me. I entitled them because I was entitled.

Entitlement didn't start with my kids. It began with me. *I entitled them* because I was entitled.

I saw just how big the world was—millions and millions of people, moms and dads with kids, just like my family, only they didn't seem to be entitled to anything, not even enough food for the day or clean water to drink. I realized how small I was. I saw my glaring selfish tendencies and my spoiled nature, and I wanted to live differently.

That discovery led my family and me on a wild faith adventure of saying yes to God in seemingly impossible ways by helping girls and women trapped in a cycle of violence and poverty. Honestly, I wouldn't have chosen this road for my family— I am entirely too afraid and selfish. But I wouldn't change our journey for all the money in the world because it's given my family the valuable gift of perspective, which reveals our deep need for gratitude, no matter what we have or don't have.

WANTS VS. NEEDS

I don't always know how to combat the struggle against entitlement in my life or home, but I need to try.

And as uncomfortable as it sounds, parents who want less-entitled kids have to be less entitled themselves, and parents who want to raise more grateful kids need to start by living more grateful lives.

As Americans, my family and I do have certain entitlements that are found in the Declaration of Independence: "We hold these truths to be self-evident, that all men are created equal, that they are endowed by their Creator with certain unalienable Rights, that among these are Life, Liberty, and the pursuit of Happiness.—That to secure these rights, Governments are instituted among Men."[5]

Joshua Becker, author of the popular blog *Becoming Minimalist*, says,

> As Americans, we are free to pursue our own happiness—however we decide to define it. . . . And those of us who have chosen to define happiness and security apart from $250K mortgages and SUVs in the garage are free to do so. Because there are greater and more important pursuits available to us than material possessions.[6]

When we pare down what we have a right to, besides what we've acquired through citizenship—which cost people their lives—the list is small. The gifts of salvation, grace, and forgiveness are free for the taking, but they weren't cheap. They cost Jesus His life.

Considering the issue as parents, what are our children entitled to? What exactly do we owe them? What is too much or not enough? Are they entitled to the latest technology, a new car at sixteen, or a fully paid college education? Some would say yes—these are the responsibilities that come with parenting.

One day in the car, my oldest, who was barely a tween at the time, overheard Terrell and me talking about Mercy House, our nonprofit ministry that funds a maternity home in Kenya. We were contemplating some pretty serious financial decisions for the future. It must have made her think because she asked me, "Mom, what is your plan for my college education?"

Parents who want to raise more grateful kids need to start by living more grateful lives.

"Well, it went to Africa," I said, laughing. "I'm joking, but honestly, we don't have plans to foot the bill for four years of college, honey. You will get a college education if you want it and work hard for it. It will happen with a combination of scholarships, work study, local summer school, and your dad and I contributing what we can too."

Madison is a gifted flute player. Years before, at the advice of her school flute teacher, we bought Madison a professional flute, paying more money than we wanted to. The teacher urged us to invest in our daughter's musical gift even if we didn't have college figured out. Since the sixth grade, Madison has known that college scholarships are part of the plan. It has spurred on her love for music. But it's also been a tangible reminder that college is not a free ride in our house.

I believe Gary Chapman and Arlene Pellicane, coauthors of *Growing Up Social*, zero in on something that is inarguable.

The only thing a child is really entitled to is his parents' love. Not to keep up with the Joneses. Not a brand new bike or iPad. Just love. Every child deserves to be loved by his or her parents. If a child has your unconditional love, he has the greatest asset in the world. If we as parents can realize it's love that our children need most, and not things, we will stop trying to buy our children's happiness with possessions.[7]

Whatever you choose to provide for your kids is really up to you. The answer will be different for every family. But when our kids begin to expect—even demand—more than our love, that's when we have a problem.

And it goes well beyond pro-viding and pursuing material possessions. What our culture feels entitled to isn't just stuff.

When our kids begin to expect—even demand—more than our love, that's when we have a problem.

It's the desire to fit in, to feel good or happy all the time; it's the desire for instant gratification and the demand to receive something just because we want it, hard work optional.

One of my kids really struggled for a season with the idea of being happy all the time. This child is more of a pessimist by nature (and so much like me), and it became obvious that when my child didn't feel happy, we saw more negative behavior. It takes consistent teaching to remember we aren't owed happiness all the time. That's not our goal because God can use disappointments and even discouragement to draw us closer to Him. Contentment is our aim because it doesn't fluctuate with our circumstances.

In their book *The Entitlement Trap*, authors Richard and Linda Eyre pinpoint the growing problem.

> Kids grow up in a reality-show world, thinking of themselves as the central character on the stage. They have a Facebook page, they are famous in their own minds, they are like rock stars, and to them there is no room (and no need) for true emotional empathy, or self-examination, or personal responsibility. Nor is there incentive or motivation to learn to work. And they think they are entitled *not* to have limits or boundaries or discipline.[8]

Early on, we chose not to allow our kids to interact on social media until they entered high school. Even after they were allowed to open accounts, we didn't encourage it and monitored their involvement. I think our resistance impacted them, and they are selective about social media. But society is in the age of unbridled and often unmonitored technology. Sometimes it's because we parents are afraid to say no or we don't want our children to feel left out. But it doesn't take a rocket scientist to recognize that parenting has changed since we were kids.

Terrell loves telling our kids the story of when he was eleven years old and desperately wanted a ten-speed bike. His parents bought him exactly what he wanted. And then a couple of months later, after the release of the hit movie *E.T.*, BMX bikes were all the rage. Terrell asked his parents for another bike. They told him, "If you want another bike, you'll have to earn the money and buy it yourself." It took him a year of sweeping his dad's print shop to earn $112 for the bike. To this day, he still speaks fondly about that bike.

The book I referenced in the introduction, *Too Much of a Good Thing*, was based on a poll and study in 2001 called "The Parenting Practices at the Millennium." Its author, Dan Kindlon, gathered data, interviewed, and studied behaviors of advantaged kids and their parents, teachers, and administrators from all over the United States. I found his research and results fascinating, some of which I will share throughout this book.

While I respect Kindlon's work greatly, his study was written fifteen years ago from a secular worldview. Although I don't claim to be an expert like Dr. Kindlon and my research isn't scientific, I thought it would be wise to ask my own questions from a more current Christian worldview. In the fall of 2014, I surveyed more than 5,000 parents from all over the country and have included that information in this book too.

When I asked parents to check off what their kids own (3,316 chose to answer this question), these were the results:

74 percent have an iPod or Kindle
55 percent have a cell phone
30 percent have a television in their room
35 percent have a personal laptop or computer
16 percent have a car of their own
5 percent have a debit or credit card for their parent's account.

There are many unknown variables—such as ages, whether or not the kids bought items themselves, and so forth—but the fact remains that our kids have a lot of stuff we didn't have at their age. And it seems this stash of stuff just continues to grow, stocked mostly by indulgent parents.

I think if we want to tackle entitlement and ingratitude in our children, it comes down to us and our choices. We have to examine ourselves and begin there. After all, how can we show our kids gratitude unless we are thankful? How can we ask them to go upstream when we are caught in the whirl-pool of our culture that demands more as the goal?

I get to spend time with a lot of young moms who volunteer at Mercy House. One day, a woman named Ashley and I were talking as we sorted items to list in the online store. I was telling her how my daughter always wanted to borrow my clothes, which many see as a form of flattery. I do, too, unless I have to dig through the laundry on her bedroom floor when I want to wear them. That story led to a conversation on entitlement.

"Oh, I know what you're talking about," she said. I looked up from what I was doing, wondering what she could possibly be referring to since her three kids were just preschoolers. "I wanted to take my little girl on a special mommy-daughter date, so I arranged a babysitter for the boys. I couldn't wait to tell her about the morning I had planned. I pulled her aside and said, 'Guess what? Mommy is going to take you on a special date. We are going ice skating, and then we are going to have hot chocolate.'"

Without missing a beat, her four-year-old said, "Is that all?"

As my friend retold the story, I could hear the pain in her

voice. She immediately saw the entitlement for what it was and explained to her daughter that she should be grateful for whatever they did together. "Okay," her little girl said and went off to play, without even understanding that her innocent question revealed her humanity.

Entitlement winds its course through my home, and the more I've become aware of its subtle infiltration, the more I see and hear it blatantly. *This is all I get? There's nothing else?* From ice cream serving sizes to allowances, the opportunity to demand more is present.

Is that all? I believe these three little words sum up the tone for those of us in most Western cultures. No one teaches us to ask that question or expect more. It's in our nature.

Just as Romans 3:23 says, "Everyone has sinned; we all fall short of God's glorious standard" (NLT). We are sinful and selfish at birth, and babies run parents ragged through long, sleepless nights demanding their needs be met immediately. But at some point, we grow up and begin to understand that the world doesn't automatically cater to our demands like our parents did. We as parents have to examine the question for ourselves, so we can say to our children with conviction, "Yes, that is all. We don't need more."

> *Is that all? I believe these three little words sum up the tone in our culture.*

As discouraging as the task of defeating entitlement in our lives may seem, I'm convinced it can be done. We can turn the tide in our homes and go against the climate in our culture by teaching a more powerful learned behavior— gratitude—that we will spend a lot of time unpacking in the coming chapters. It might sound simplistic, but I believe the cure to our kids wanting more starts with teaching them to be thankful for what they already have.

GOING AGAINST THE FLOW

Parents

> Ask God to reveal to you your own entitlement issues. It's the best place to start.
> In what areas of your life do you struggle with entitlement? Do you put expectations on your spouse or friends or even your children?
> Keep a gratitude journal, getting kids to participate too. Or write down the highs from your day and put them in a container at your table. Choose random times to pull out the slips of paper and reflect on the good things in your life.

Toddlers/Preschoolers

> This is the perfect age to begin teaching gratitude. Toddlers and preschoolers are all about mimicking our behavior. We can show them gratitude by displaying it to our spouses and to them.
> Color pictures and give them as thank-you notes to others.

Elementary

> Write blessings on sticky notes and put them on a mirror or fill up a whole window as a family with jotted-down gratitude.

> Begin the process of connecting work with reward. Consider putting a job board in the kitchen. It's a great way to begin teaching kids the correlation between hard work and earning money, and it's a great way to counteract entitlement.

Tweens/Teens

> Make your expectations clear. If you've noticed an attitude of entitlement in your tween/teen, talk with him or her about your expectations. Don't believe the lie that it is too late. If your teen isn't contributing, let him or her know what you expect.

> Don't engage in a battle. You might need to give reminders and reinforcements of your requirement if it's new. If your older child won't cooperate, use Dr. Kevin Leman's strategy that B (something your son or daughter wants to do) doesn't happen until A (something you want him or her to do) is completed.

> Give your tween/teen the gift of listening. At this age, more than anything, your child wants you to hear him or her (which is different from understanding or even agreeing with your teen).

CHAPTER 2

TIMES HAVE
CERTAINLY CHANGED

TERRELL AND I ARE big fans of *The Andy Griffith Show*. There have been nights when we have had a mini–Mayberry marathon, watching half a dozen episodes in a row. We are wild, aren't we? There's just something about the good old days. Plus, I've always had a thing for Andy.

An alternative title to this book might be *Everything I've Ever Learned about Parenting Came from "The Andy Griffith Show."* Sheriff Taylor's wisdom is pure gold. One of our favorite episodes is "Opie and the Spoiled Kid."

Opie's friend Arnold Winkler rides over to the Taylors' house to show off his new expensive bike. When Arnold offers to give Opie a ride on the fancy Intercontinental Flyer,

Opie politely turns him down. He has chores to finish so he can get his weekly quarter.

Arnold can't believe Opie has to *work* for his measly allowance and proceeds to school Opie on what Sheriff Taylor owes his son. "He's taking advantage of ya," Arnold says. "What do you think 'allowance' means? It means money a kid is *allowed* to have. And without working for it. It's for being a kid."

The argument is convincing. Opie not only asks his dad for a fifty-cent raise in his allowance, but also announces that he expects the weekly amount without doing any work in return. Andy doesn't budge.

Arnold advises Opie to take action with temper tantrums, with plenty of kicking and crying. "And if that doesn't work, you hold your breath to get your way," says Arnold. It's a lot for Opie to think about.

In the next scene, Arnold rides his bike on the sidewalk after being warned that it is against the law, and the bike is impounded. Arnold stomps off to tell his dad, and a few minutes later Opie arrives at the sheriff's office to take the allowance discussion to the next level. Try as he might, Opie's tantrums and manipulation have no effect on Andy at all.

When Arnold brings his dad to see Sheriff Taylor and demand his bike back, Arnold's true colors are shown and his dad sees them for the first time.[1]

The episode ends with Opie asking for his job back and apologizing for the way he acted. And yes, Andy even gives him a raise.

If you ask me, that show illustrates parenting at its finest. I know we can't recapture those iconic black-and-white television days that our parents or grandparents experienced. Our world has evolved into a modern, state-of-the-art society and Mayberry is history, but some days I wish we could go back to a time when life seemed simpler.

When the back-to-school season hit at the end of last summer, humorist and blogger Victoria Fedden wrote a hilarious post titled "Going Back to School: The 70s vs. Today" that went viral.[2]

I've excerpted a little of it here:

BACK TO SCHOOL, 1970s

> Take the kids downtown to go shopping at Sears for back-to-school clothes the last week of August. Get everyone a new pair of corduroys and a striped tee shirt. Buy the boys a pair of dungarees and the girls a pair of culottes. No, Jennifer, you can't have that orange-and-red poncho. Promise you will crochet her a better one with much more fringe. Get the girls a package of that rainbow, fuzzy yarn they like in their hair. You are done. You have spent a total of $43.00. Now take everyone to the Woolworth's lunch counter for grilled cheeses and chocolate milk.

> On the night before the first day of school (that would be the Sunday night after Labor Day, of course, you know, mid-September) throw the kids in the way back of the station wagon and drag them downtown to Eckerds, K-Mart, Ames, Dollar General, Drug Fair, or the like and hurry them over to the back-to-school area to pick out a lunchbox . . .

BACK TO SCHOOL, 2014

> Take five deep breaths and say a positive affirmation. School begins in two weeks. It is the middle of July. Don't worry, you still have time to order BPA-free bento boxes and authentic Indian tiffins made with special stainless steel that did not involve any child-labor, sweat shops or animal cruelty. Remember, you have Amazon Prime . . .

> Begin frantic online search for backpacks and school bags made from all-natural materials yet still "cool." Have them monogrammed.

> Take kids shopping at the mall for new school clothes. Buy them each a completely new wardrobe from Gymboree and Crew Cuts. Spend $2,387.07 on your credit card.

It's as if our culture has amped up life and made things more complicated, not because we have to but because we can. We have the time and money to focus and care deeply about things that really don't matter.

Kids will be kids and if we give them too much, too soon, they will likely take it.

Yes, times have changed. But kids really haven't. Entitled kids have been around since God created human beings. So maybe it's the parenting that has changed the most. Maybe we are giving our kids more than they need and allowing them to have all they want with few consequences. Because—let's admit it—kids will be kids and if we give them too much, too soon, they will likely take it.

TWO FAVORITE SONS

There are plenty of father-son stories in the Bible, but let's look at two sons in particular: Joseph, the son of Jacob, and Absalom, one of David's sons. Joseph's life story is found in Genesis 37–50, and in the first few verses of the narration we learn that Joseph was deeply loved by his father (Genesis 37:3), causing his ten older brothers to be jealous, and that Joseph was also a tattletale (verse 2) who informed his father about the bad things his brothers were doing behind their father's back.

To make matters worse, Jacob had a beautiful coat made for Joseph, and when his brothers saw the coat "they hated him and could not speak a kind word to him" (Genesis 37:4). Joseph added fuel to the fire when he told his brothers about his dreams, which basically implied he would rule over them one day. While the dreams eventually turned out to be prophetic, Joseph's decision to share them wasn't the best move. Even if you aren't familiar with this story, you could probably guess what happened next: His brothers were furious, hated him even more than before, and plotted revenge. They faked Joseph's death and then sold him into slavery. Which really puts perspective on my kids' silly sibling rivalry, you know?

But thankfully, the story doesn't end there. No, like most of God's stories for us, this one ends in amazing redemption. Joseph continued being faithful to God, living a life of integrity, and was placed in the highest command just under Pharaoh. When a drought devastated Egypt, it was Joseph's organization and forethought that saved the nation, including the brothers who bullied him (Genesis 41:41-57).

Fast-forward seven hundred years. King David was the

ruler of Israel and his third son, Absalom, had an extreme case of entitlement. Many biblical commentaries say Absalom was more than spoiled—he was a narcissist, with an oversized ego fed by his vanity and selfishness. When I read in 2 Samuel 13–18 about this favored royal son who murdered his brother Amnon for raping their sister, led a revolt against his father, King David, and in the process raped his father's concubines in plain sight, I don't feel my family is quite as dysfunctional as I feared. Absalom was used to getting what he wanted.

Certainly, David demonstrated some serious flaws in his parenting. Besides favoring Absalom, he did not restrain or properly discipline his children, especially noticeable after Amnon raped his sister. Instead of David placing a crown on his son Absalom's head, the father and son became enemies in the eyes of David's government leaders, and Absalom died trying to escape his father's men (2 Samuel 18:9-15).

Here are two men in the Bible, both favored and spoiled as children, but we see two completely different outcomes. I'm not a Bible scholar, and I don't really know why one turned out to be a hero who saved thousands while the other was killed in the rebellion he led against his own father. But I do believe that it boils down to two things: absolute truth and personal choice.

ABSOLUTE TRUTH

Before we became parents, Terrell and I were youth and children's pastors. We poured our lives into the kids in our care, giving them a Christian education. Our favorite resource back then was Josh McDowell's book *Right from Wrong*. He helped us lead our students in knowing and understanding that there are absolute truths in our world. The premise of the book defines absolute truth as this:

> When you believe there exists an objective standard for distinguishing right from wrong—that certain things are right for all people, for all times, for all places—you acknowledge that there are fundamental moral and ethical guidelines that exist independently of your personal opinion.[3]

Today's society argues that truth is subjective; truth changes to accommodate our opinions. Let me give you an example. An absolute truth—a standard of right or wrong for all people, at all times, for all places—would be that murder is wrong. But society says it's okay if it's an unborn baby. We've taken an absolute truth and changed it to fit a situation for the sake of convenience.

When we look closely at Absalom's life, we can see that he didn't believe in the moral truths that God set as a standard for all people, at all times, in all situations. He sought revenge and murdered a man, raped women, and usurped his father's authority as king because it fulfilled his purpose, not God's. In contrast, Joseph, who was sold into slavery, was enticed by his superior's wife to sleep with her. But rather than go against one of God's moral standards, Joseph fled. Instead of being lauded for his actions, Joseph was falsely accused of immorality and imprisoned. Joseph chose to do the right thing because he understood right from wrong and chose truth even if it meant consequences he didn't deserve.

I've seen the shift from truth in our culture in a variety of ways, from what's on TV to what's in books. What used to be taboo is now socially acceptable. What used to be wrong is now right in some circumstances. It's hard to find a book in the teenage section of the library that doesn't have same-sex couples, intimate sexual scenes, or offensive language once reserved for "R" ratings.

My son unknowingly brought home a book with questionable content in the sixth grade. After reading a couple of chapters, he tapped on our bedroom door, well past his bedtime. As soon as I saw his expression, I knew something was bothering him.

"What's wrong?" I asked.

"It's this book that we're supposed to read for class. I started it, but there are things that make me uncomfortable. I don't want to read it."

I was so proud of him, and I e-mailed the teacher on his behalf. She was quick to offer an alternative book. My son could have continued to read the first one. Many of us have probably watched a movie or read a book with content that went against our moral standards. I'm not saying either is wrong, but seeing that my son was uncomfortable with something that went against the absolute truths he embraces—and risking other people knowing it—made me take notice.

Society has shifted truth by bombarding us with an idea until it's normalized.

Society has shifted truth by bombarding us with an idea until it's normalized. People eventually accept it as truth because others do or because culture calls it politically correct to do so. We call it tolerance, which makes my version of the truth as valid as yours. When you push against this new "truth," you are marginalized.

When Americans were asked by the Barna Research Group if absolute truth exists, more surprising than the results was how much and how quickly the results changed in just a few years. In 1995, 50 percent of born-again Christians said there were moral truths that are unchanging, and that truth is absolute, not relative to the circumstances. In 2000, another poll showed the number of respondents who agreed with those statements was up to 53 percent. Again, the same question was asked in 2009 and 2015, and the survey found that 46 percent believe that moral truth is absolute. The same research group found that among teenagers, 83 percent said moral truth depends on situational truth.

All we have to do is turn on the news or see a magazine cover to see this playing out in our culture. Truth is constantly changing in our world. What once used to be wrong and totally taboo is now a boldface tabloid headline. Why does it matter? Our kids' worldview is based on what truth they believe, and they make choices from that filter. If they are taught a biblical worldview, they will learn that absolute truth exists based on the Bible's principles, but if we allow our culture to teach them, they will have a secular worldview that continues to redefine truth based on their feelings or circumstances. If we don't teach our kids right from wrong, they will learn the version presented by the media.

Honestly, I wasn't prepared to talk to my teens about Bruce Jenner becoming Caitlyn Jenner for the world to see and applaud. But I could hardly hide it from them either.

Kids are talking about what the world is talking about, and so we must broach these difficult topics. We were driving in the car when I overheard my kids talking about it. "What do y'all think of this?" I asked.

"I think it's really weird," my son said. My daughter agreed.

"How do you think God feels about this?" I asked.

We didn't solve all the world's problems that day and we didn't understand what would cause someone to make this kind of choice, but it was a great opportunity to reestablish what the Bible says about how God created us and how to love people we don't agree with. Still, it was uncomfortable looking at the cover of *Vanity Fair* featuring Caitlyn Jenner with my kids when we saw it at the checkout line.

We won't show people Jesus with our list of rules; we will be known by our love for each other.

In another report that examined the changes in worldview among Christians in a 2009 survey, the Barna Group stated, "A person's worldview is primarily shaped and is firmly in place by the time someone reaches the age of 13; it is refined through experience during the teen and early adult years; and then it is passed on to others during their adult life."[4]

I don't write this to discourage us, but rather to remind us that it's our job to teach our kids what truth is. I love how Josh McDowell explains the reason behind truth in *Right from Wrong*:

God's Word is filled with PRECEPTS—commands put there for our good. [Ex: "Do not murder"

protects people from being killed.] PRINCIPLES are
the "whys" behind the precepts [We don't murder
because God gives life and there are consequences
for committing murder], and the PERSON behind
the principles is God Himself [God is creator of
life, therefore, God values life]. As we move from
PRECEPT to PRINCIPLE, it leads to the very
PERSON of God. It is through the Test of Truth
that we compare our attitudes and actions to God's
character and nature.[5]

We must teach our kids that there are clear absolute truths
that not only protect us—they also provide for us. But without love, they are just a big list of rules. I think the church as
a whole has forgotten the two greatest commandments—to
love God and to love others (Matthew 22:36-40). It's easy to
love people like us, those who embrace our beliefs. But it's
even more important to love those who aren't like us, people
who don't live by absolute truth. We won't show people
Jesus with our list of rules; we will be known by our love
for each other. Ultimately, we want them to see the person
behind our love.

A new commandment I give to you, that you love
one another, even as I have loved you, that you
also love one another. By this all men will know
that you are My disciples, if you have love for one
another.

JOHN 13:34-35, NASB

31

When we decide to follow Christ, we are choosing a narrow path. It's not an easy road to live out the gospel, as author David Platt states at the beginning of his book *Counter Culture.*

> The gospel is the lifeblood of Christianity, and it provides the foundation for *countering culture.* For when we truly believe the gospel, we begin to realize that the gospel not only *compels* Christians to confront social issues in the culture around us. The gospel actually *creates* confrontation with the culture around—and within—us.[6]

I don't know about you, but I say, "Bring it on."

PERSONAL CHOICE

The second thing I believe made Joseph a hero and Absalom a zero was personal choice.

A couple of summers ago, Madison went on a local missions trip with her youth group. They spent three nights and four days serving lunch at a homeless shelter, stacking food at the Houston Food Bank, and volunteering at a day care for low-income families. She returned exhausted, dirty, and with a lot of questions that took us by surprise. My kids have seen a lot in their short years. We've exposed them to extreme poverty in other countries and in our own city. They have seen suffering and understand in their core that life can be very unfair.

As I listened to Madison wrestle with questions that I have also asked myself—"Why does God allow this?" "What if He doesn't still speak today?" "Is it okay if I don't want to be a missionary?"—I tried to help by telling her what I believed. But Terrell cautioned me that while it was uncomfortable to hear our firstborn ask hard questions, they weren't mine to answer. I knew in my heart we had to let her figure them out for herself. It was tempting to tell her what to think and what to believe just because it's what her dad and I believe. But I knew if we allowed her to struggle with her questions and gave her freedom to ask them, she would become stronger in her beliefs in the end.

I can honestly say, this is hard ground for a parent. When I peeled back the layers, I discovered I was afraid for her to ask hard questions because I feared she would choose wrongly. I went to Madison later and apologized for not trusting her. I explained how hard it was for me to let her grow up and question everything—from our authority to her faith—but I had to let her. I had to trust God that we had done our part in teaching her, but most difficult for me, I had to believe in my daughter. My reward was seeing the relief on her face. The funny thing is, Madison didn't make any life-changing decisions that day. She's still the same Jesus-loving girl, trying her best to live for Him, but she knows that she is free to question things and make personal choices, and that experience changed both of us.

Please understand that not every single minute of every day in our family is weighted with intention or a Is-This-a-Good–Decision? conversation. We also have a lot of fun together. We are silly and often irreverent and unholy. I started my blog in 2007 with the tag line, "We are a lot like the *Family Circus* cartoon, only with more trips to the emergency room" for that very reason. Don't think for a minute that intentional living equals holiness. It really just means we are aiming for the stars but lucky if we hit a street lamp.

Without a doubt, one of the most helpful things in this parenting journey has been learning from other moms who are further down the road than I am, women who freely share their successes and regrets. Lee, who is old enough to be my mother, is one of those people. She dropped by one day and brought me a couple of photocopied articles that her husband, Trace, thought I might like to read. Trace is a theologian and former seminary professor with degrees in Greek and Hebrew, as well as law, so he knows his stuff.

As Lee and I talked, she pointed to the underlined words on the pages and said, "You know that verse in Proverbs that says, 'Train up a child in the way he should go, and when he is old he will not depart from it'?"[7]

"Oh yes," I said, nodding in agreement. "I claim that Scripture over my kids all the time."

"Well, I did too," she said. "Only it doesn't mean what we think it does at all. I wish I'd known this earlier."

After Lee left, I curled up on my bed and spread out the papers. The first pages were from the book *Basics of Biblical Hebrew Grammar* by Gary D. Pratico and Miles V. Van Pelt. As I scanned down the page, I could see the underlined verse written in Hebrew with the explanation of each word underneath. The authors suggest that "in the way he should go" could more accurately be translated as "according to his way" and note that this Scripture is actually a solemn warning rather than a promise. It doesn't mean that our kids will always stay on the path we have taught them to follow or that if they stray they will eventually return to the faith.

Instead, Pratico and Van Pelt come to a startling conclusion.

Parents, if you train up your child "according to *his* way"—in other words, if you quit the hard work of loving discipline and just give in and let your child have his own way—you will reinforce his sinful proclivities to such a degree that, apart from supernatural intervention, "even when is old he will not depart from it."[8]

Profound, isn't it? This verse, say the authors, is actually warning parents against doing something they should not do: "train up a child in his way." This was revolutionary and enlightening to me. As I began to process what that meant, I picked up the second article, one from *Bibliotheca Sacra*, which confirmed what I had just read.

"Train a child according to his evil inclinations and he will continue in his evil way throughout his life." . . . It says, in other words, not "Here's the good result that you can count on when you give a child proper parental guidance," but "Here's the bad result that may happen if you *don't* give a child proper parental guidance, but let him do what *he* wants."[9]

Pratico adds,

As desirable as such a promise [offered by the more common interpretation] would be, experience contradicts it far too often to be attributable solely to deficient parenting. Indeed, in spite of the best parenting in the universe, namely God's own, many

of his children departed from the way they should
have gone, and they continued in their rebellion
to the bitter end (cf. Isaiah 1:2 "I reared children
and brought them up, but they have rebelled
against me").[11]

Talk about instant deflation. I had always clung to that
verse as a promise: Do this faithfully and this is what will
happen. Who doesn't want to claim that promise over their
children? Promises like that are comforting, especially in
seasons when our kids are rebellious or wayward. But as I
reflected further, I realized that I was already heeding this
warning in Scripture by offering my kids parental guidance
and not letting them do everything they want.

Kids often learn things the hard way. But God uses mistakes, wayward choices, and brokenness to bring redemption.

Do you know what this does?
It takes a load off. How many
families do we know, maybe even
our own, who have a couple of
kids serving God but also one
who has abandoned everything he has been taught? Proverbs
assures us that our responsibility is to faithfully do our part
to explain the truth, and the rest is up to our child. Each
person must individually make the choice to follow Jesus.
And while it may grieve us deeply when this doesn't happen,
we can hold firmly to the knowledge that we obeyed God
and followed through on our responsibilities. And we can
find great comfort in knowing that God loves our children
even more than we do and He will continue to pursue them.

Here's the truth: Kids often choose the wrong path and

learn things the hard way. Sure, they could avoid pain and heartache if they would just listen to us, but this is part of growing up. At some point we have to let them. God often uses mistakes, wayward choices, and brokenness to bring redemption. We have to entrust our children to Him and pray they ultimately choose Him, as Joseph did.

My kids love to read, and it has been a challenge to find them age-appropriate books. It's been tempting to nix a lot of the popular fiction on the bestseller lists because of suggestive content. A couple of years ago when *The Fault in Our Stars* was The Book To Read, both my teen daughter and I read it, even though I knew the main characters engaged in premarital sex. After we finished, we talked about the choices the characters in the book made. Sometimes I think we parents are so focused on saying no and following all the rules to raise great kids that we miss the opportunity for an important conversation on why we say no.

We've done the same thing with a lot of other books. We've spent years teaching our kids right from wrong and living by absolute truths, but at some point, we have to let them begin to make decisions on their own. It's not easy and we definitely mess up, but we are trying.

For example, I like our house to be clean and clutter-free. That sounds nice on paper, but it's code for obsessive-compulsive tendencies. When the house is a mess, I feel like a mess inside and I go into overdrive. We all know children and messes go together, but my kids know I'm a nicer person when things are tidy. Jon-Avery was helping me with dinner one night, and as he began to pour a bottle of dressing into the dish, he completely missed and it covered the countertop and the cabinets beneath, and dripped to the floor. I lost it and yelled and then continued to gripe as we both attempted to clean it up.

"I'm sorry, Mom. I know you don't like it when I'm human," he said in a quiet voice.

His words were like a knife to my heart. He was helping me, and I was hurting him. A few minutes later, after we'd wiped away the mess, I knocked the entire dish off the counter.

"Mom, you should be more careful," he said kindly (but with a note of sarcasm) as he bent to pick up my mess.

I stopped what I was doing, put my hand on his, and said, "I'm sorry. Thanks for treating me better than I treated you."

I still cringe when I think of that day, but sometimes our greatest messes teach us the most about each other and ourselves.

PASSING THE BATON OF TRUTH

Recently I met an old friend for lunch and as we caught up on each other's lives, I told her I was writing this book. I added my usual disclaimer that just because I was writing a book on parenting didn't mean I knew how to parent. She laughed and said her oldest child was a young adult and she still didn't know that much about it.

"I worry about my son and his struggle with pornography." I was so glad she opened up because that's what real friends do. "He tries so hard to stay away from it, and he will go months without giving in to temptation—and then he fails. I just don't want this to be a lifelong struggle for him."

She knows my story and how my husband struggled and

overcame the same sin years ago in our marriage. "This is a weakness for your son, as well as for most young men his age and older," I replied. "Okay, probably all men. But he is struggling against it. That's good! He isn't giving himself over to it. He's trying. And when he fails, he tries again. This is life."

I told her how every time I sit down to write, I struggle with thinking the reader—*you*—would think *I think* I am an expert or I know what I'm doing. And I told her that day that I don't know how my kids are going to turn out. I don't know if one of them will make really bad choices and lead a life I wouldn't choose for him or her. I can't predict what will happen. I know that I am teaching them truth according to God's Word and loving them the best way I can by thoughtfully guiding and encouraging them, but I also have to let them make their own decisions and pray they find Jesus in their successes or failures.

And friends, that's all we can do.

GOING AGAINST THE FLOW

Parents

> Ask God for strength and determination to heed the warning given to us in Scripture to not give our kids everything they want.
> As hard as it may be, let your kids ask the hard questions. Remember, if they are asking or talking to you about faith or morality issues, there's an open door. Don't slam it shut by demanding they believe just like you do. If we let them come to their own conclusions (influenced by our counsel), we won't regret it.

> Maybe you've read this chapter and you're thinking it's too late. It's never too late to start. God can redeem anything, even time. Start with small changes. Ask God for wisdom and pray that His truth will lead you.

Toddlers/Preschoolers

> One of the best ways to teach young kids biblical truths is by repetition and example.
> Honor their good decisions to tell the truth, love others, and so forth, by recognizing and reinforcing their choices with positive rewards.
> The Hermie and Friends series by Max Lucado (books, DVDs, and board books) is a great series that introduces truth to kids.
> Start with the major stories of the Bible or a children's storybook Bible. Have fun reenacting a story and quizzing them on the outcome.

Elementary

> Teach absolute truth (e.g., lying is wrong). Make connections between truths found in the Bible and everyday life experiences.
> Explain natural consequences when we don't follow God's truth. What happens when we touch the hot stove, even when Mom says not to?
> If they are struggling in school or at home, find ways to teach them what God has to say about being discouraged or angry. Point them back to the Bible.
> We love the Adventures in Odyssey audio series, which teaches core biblical truths.

> Both volumes of *The Big Book of Bible Truths* by Sinclair Ferguson are great storytelling mediums to teach biblical truths to kids.

Tweens/Teens

> Bring up current topics that you know your kids are hearing discussed at school or by their friends. Hear them out, share your insights, and then ask, "What does the Bible say about this?"
> Read the books they are reading and watch the movies they love. If either contains suggestive or offensive language or behavior, ask, "What would you do in that situation?" "Do you think that was right or wrong?"
> Talk about an absolute truth (Principle). Look for where it's found in the Bible (Precept). Then ask, "What does that absolute truth reveal about God's nature?" (Person).

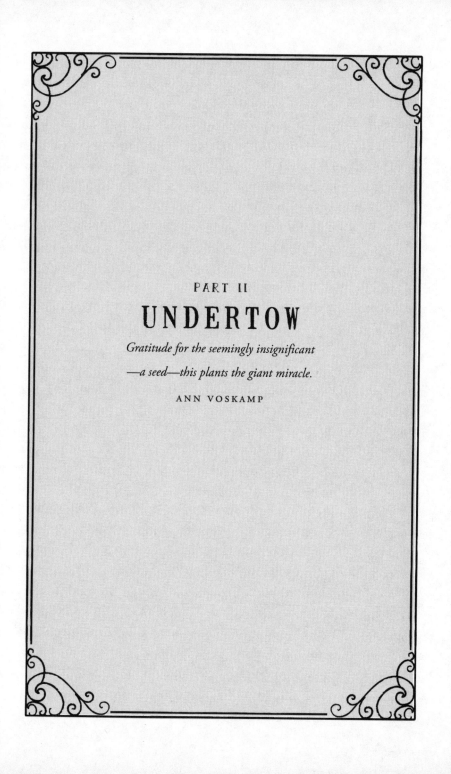

PART II

UNDERTOW

Gratitude for the seemingly insignificant
—a seed—this plants the giant miracle.

ANN VOSKAMP

CHAPTER 3

SEVEN WAYS WE PARENTS MISS THE BOAT (AND HOW TO GET ON BOARD)

WE LIVED IN a different state than our extended families for the first ten years of our marriage. Every time I would visit the town in Texas my parents settled in as empty nesters, I wanted to live there. I missed my family, but I also loved their town. It was a beautiful planned community with tall pine trees and winding sidewalks; it was family-friendly with a park on nearly every corner and boasted the best schools in the state. It was *the place* to live and raise kids outside of Houston.

When we finally moved back "home" to Texas, it wasn't because our dream was coming true. Having abruptly left full-time ministry because we were miserable, we needed jobs. My dad offered us a small, empty townhome to rent

45

until we could get on our feet. Sometimes you gratefully take what is offered to get what you want.

Madison and Jon-Avery were just toddlers when we relocated, and we were living off a meager savings account, with Terrell job hunting daily. I joined a Bible study at a new church to meet other moms and because they had free child care for the two-hour meetings. One week, the ladies started talking about the best preschools, the ones your kids *must* attend in order to be ready for school. They talked about waiting lists and registration fees and monthly tuition. I didn't say a word—I just listened. By the end of the class, my stomach was in a knot.

Worry about preschool? I didn't know it was something I needed to do. It was the first time I can remember feeling like I owed my children something I couldn't provide. And it was a terrible feeling. I loved my kids as much as my new friends did theirs, and it seemed if everyone else said preschool was a priority, I should make it one too. Even though it sounds immature and naive, that's how I spent my early parenting years—trying to give my kids everything because everyone else was. Somehow the line between what they needed and what I wanted for them blurred.

I spent many years trying to give my kids everything. The line between what they needed and what I wanted for them blurred.

I ended up working at a church part-time. In exchange, my kids could attend preschool two days a week and I was able to bring home a small amount of money. It was hardly a noteworthy education, but it was a place to start. Terrell eventually got a good job and the kids transferred to a better preschool. I signed them up for soccer and gymnastics and swim lessons and basketball. We had big birthday parties and moved to our dream home in that wooded town. We were finally just like everyone else. Well, sort of. We were just like the people we compared ourselves to.

Once my kids started elementary school, I entered an entirely new world of competitive living. Before long, I was sitting at a picnic table with other moms waiting for the afternoon bell to ring, listening to conversations about European vacations, lake-house renovations, and Ivy League college funds. By that time, I had just returned from my life-changing trip to Africa, and I became disillusioned with always trying to keep up. The little impromptu gatherings around the picnic table felt empty once I had a completely different group of people to compare myself to: new friends with much less.

Visiting an orphan-led home in Kenya just weeks before had turned my life upside down. That's where I met Vincent. I will never forget standing in Vincent's home, which was the size of my master closet. Water dripped on my head in the dark room as he lit a candle and explained how he walked an hour to school each way and cared for his little brother because his parents were both dead. As he told us about his life, he smiled from ear to ear with joy.

"How can you be so happy?" I asked as I looked around at all he didn't have.

"I have Jesus. He is enough," he answered confidently.

His answer was my undoing. Because I had Jesus, too, but He wasn't enough for me. I wanted more—more money, more stuff, more to fill the emptiness.

That's the day I started my quest for contentment and found it not in building my American Dream, but in giving it away.

Returning to my little world, I was surrounded by people who wanted the best of everything—cars, homes, education, jobs—and it didn't take long for us to join them. But now my kids felt it too—this pressure to keep up and be like everyone else. They didn't want to be the deprived ones. They didn't want to feel different. That's what happens when you live in a place where everyone is just like you. You begin to compare yourself to those you're around, and that becomes your world. It had happened to me, and now I was watching it happen to my kids. Suddenly, my third grader and first grader were asking for certain brands of clothes, lavish toys, and expensive electronics. They wanted what they saw everyone else had. I had fed the entitlement beast, and now it was hungry for more.

In my 2014 parenting poll, when I asked parents if they felt their kids acted entitled at times, a whopping 93 percent said yes. This anonymous comment really stood out to me: "My kids think that certain benefits will be afforded them based on what they see peers receiving for nothing. Their statements of expectation are both naive and straightforward. They don't question that they will receive a smartphone or a car someday; they believe it is a right of childhood, based on their experience in the world."

In the less than 7 percent who didn't feel their kids were entitled, several parents answered, "Aren't we all?" And still others answered that "selfishness is the American way." Their comments made me realize that in some ways we *expect* our kids to be selfish. It's part of our sin nature that others refer to simply as human nature. It's our job to teach our children to be different from their natural bent toward sin.

In her series of posts on "'Stuff,' Satisfaction, and the Suburban Child," blogger and Bible teacher Jen Wilkin says,

> We moved to the suburbs, like most young families, because they were affordably safe. . . .
>
> Our suburban neighbors—with the help of dual incomes, starting families later in life, smaller family sizes, and ample credit limits—are able to afford much more than physical safety for themselves and their children. Hence, the first grader with the cell phone, the fourth grader with the iTouch, the seventh grader with the $300 purse and professionally colored hair, the sixteen-year-old with the Mustang GT. The clothes, vacations, parties, electronics, and activities which surround the suburban child make our own childhoods look downright deprived, but most parents are happy to forget that stripped-down upbringing. They take satisfaction in knowing that they have given their children more than was given to them.
>
> Ironically, the affordable safety of the suburbs turns out to be neither affordable nor safe. The price tag for chasing our children's material desires will be far higher than the total on our credit card statements. As Christian parents, we must think clearly about what our spending patterns teach our children.[1]

When I was in sixth grade, I remember I wanted a pair of Guess jeans more than I wanted my mom to stop giving me home perms. Jeans were status. They were the key to fitting in at school, or so I thought. I begged and pleaded, but my parents wouldn't—and probably couldn't—fork over the fifty dollars to make me happy. Instead my mom bought me an off-brand look-alike pair, with a similar triangle patch on the back pocket. But instead of the word *Guess* on the patch, my knockoff pair had the word *Tropics*. So I did what every desperate twelve-year-old girl does—I took a black Sharpie marker and wrote Guess over Tropics, which looked just as bad as you'd imagine. My mom made me wear them until I outgrew them.

That's the memory that sometimes surfaces when my kids ask me for something they don't need and we probably can't afford or shouldn't buy. I remembered those jeans when Madison started asking for jeans by the brand, and I thought about how embarrassing it was to wear them. *I don't ever want my kids to feel that way*, I thought. But I realized I was on dangerous ground. Because with this mindset, the only way to protect them is to give them everything they want.

It's our duty to give our kids what they need—food, shelter, and love—and oftentimes, we are able to give them much more than that.

Now I try to remember what I learned from that fashion disaster: I was ungrateful that my mom tried to help by buying the knockoff version she could afford; I was wasteful for damaging a good pair of jeans that I ended up having to wear; and in the long run, I survived and learned some valuable lessons. Plus, a couple of months later, my parents surprised my sister and me by splurging on gold lamé fabric jackets with a blue shiny star on the back. It was the Michael Jackson era. Cool points.

As parents, I think it's our duty to give our kids what they need—food, shelter, and love—and oftentimes, we are able to give them much more than that. But it's in our nature to want to give them what we can't always provide: happiness.

WHY PARENTS DO WHAT THEY KNOW THEY SHOULDN'T

We don't just overindulge our kids with excessive stuff. We also tend to give in to whims and demands, allowing too much freedom too soon. Our kids are being exposed to "more, quicker, now" than ever before, and we have to ask why. I think it's partly because of easy access to the Internet and overexposure to media. We have the world—good and bad—at our fingertips. Kids are handed touch screen devices as toddlers. They learn about sex on Google and grow up watching episodes of *Teen Mom* and *16 and Pregnant*. Why does our society indulge our kids so much? Why do we as their parents give in when we know we shouldn't? Besides wanting them to have what we didn't, I think we overindulge our kids for a variety of reasons.

We Want Our Kids to Be Our Friends

I love spending time with my kids. They are smart and funny and make me laugh. Like the first day of school a couple of years ago. We have a first-and-last-day-of-school tradition. After the first day of school each year, we drive half an hour to The Candy Store, which is run by a little old man. I hold my breath every year, hoping that the store is still open because when I say old, I mean it.

I ran into a good friend on one of these celebratory days, and as we talked I boasted about my kids and their good choices and how they loved Jesus. About that time, I turned around to the commotion they were making, and all three of them were "smoking" candy cigarettes.

"Take a picture of us smoking, Mom!" my youngest yelled. I sheepishly shrugged at my friend. We bought several packs and enjoyed them all the way home.

Yes, one minute we are laughing at a joke during dinner and then the next minute it gets out of hand—someone has *become* the joke and it needs to stop. Terrell and I have a choice to make: friend or authority? Dan Kindlon offers some guidance.

> We want to talk things out with our kids, reason
> with them, rather than impose authoritarian
> punishments such as taking away privileges; we want
> open and honest communication, not dictatorial
> rule. This philosophy has both benefits and risks.
> We want to be emotionally close to our kids, to have
> fun with them, to be, to some extent, their friends.
> This blurring of the line between being a friend and
> being a parent is one of the most significant trends
> in parenting today, and it often results in confusion
> for us and our kids.[2]

He goes on to say that with the high divorce rate, kids often become our friends. Or when marriages and jobs become frustrating, our time with our child can make us feel better.

> But if we spoil our children with material goods in order to get a hug, or fail to set appropriate limits out of fear that they will withdraw their love or be upset, we have burdened them with protecting us from unhappiness.[3]

The bottom line? Kids aren't meant to be our friends until they are independent of us.

We Are Afraid to Say No Because of the Fallout

Let's be honest—some of our kids are more "passionate" than others. There have been moments in my home when I actually felt afraid to be the authority figure. The moment passed, thankfully, because one of us had to be in charge, and we all know how it turns out when we let our kids assume that role. But I was afraid, because I knew the minute I said *no* or *you can't*, there would be tears and, well, fallout. We've had our fair share of doors slamming, eyes rolling, and shouting. But we all know the opposite of saying no or not saying anything is saying yes, you can have your way or do what you want.

We Feel Guilty about Our Circumstances

Whether it's divorce, remarriage, job changes, or just a really bad day, sometimes we let our situation influence our parenting. And in our weakness, we give too much or give in too soon. The term "mom guilt" probably rings a bell for many of you; I've had my fair share of struggling with it.

When my youngest, Emerson, was in first grade, I told her I would come to lunch at her school. I ended up having a crazy, unexpected morning, and when I looked at the clock, her lunchtime was starting and I was still at home. I rushed to the school with a thrown-together lunch and spent the rest of the day trying to make it up to her (which she had no problem letting me do).

Occasionally, she refers to "that time you almost forgot me" and I have to push the guilt away. I tell her that life is sometimes unpredictable and remind her that I did eventually show up, pathetic lunch and all.

We Are Busy

Hectic lives and busy schedules affect the way we parent. Some days it's just easier to hit the drive-through for dinner again or hand our toddler our phone so we can keep shopping. But being too busy all the time tends to make us depend on shortcuts. Convenience can help us, but it also changes the way we parent over time. It can easily become the norm and, even more, an expectation. When Madison started high school, Jon-Avery started junior high, which meant early mornings for Emerson, who was still in elementary school. Yes, three car trips in different directions. Terrell would take Madison one way, and I would drag Emerson out of bed to accompany me as we dropped off her brother at his school. Some days Terrell and I switched it up.

One morning I stopped by Chick-fil-A for a quick breakfast because we were running late, not knowing Terrell had done the same thing with his passenger the day before. Guess who asked for a special breakfast every day for the rest of the week?

Being busy is a by-product of our culture in so many ways. And I'm busier now with our nonprofit, Mercy House, than I've ever been. But I think the real danger is when we are busy with things that don't matter, like helping our kids keep up with what everyone else has or focusing on helping our kids be the best at their sport or hobby even if it sacrifices every opportunity for meals together with the family. When we work long hours to pay for more lessons and bigger houses, better cars and more stuff, it's easy to get lost in a cycle of busyness.

We Don't Want Them to Fail

Every school year brings a new learning curve for our family. As my kids have gotten older, their schedules have become more demanding and exhausting. My kids are cut from the same cloth as I am—they tend to be overachievers and thrive on being challenged. About two months into the school year, one of my kids asked me to buy a copy of one of the great classics for a class project. A library copy wouldn't work because of the need to highlight text and write notes in it.

The only problem was that my child got the date wrong for when the assignment was due so the book was needed in two days. We had a busy week with out-of-country guests and meetings, so I ordered it on Amazon and paid a couple of extra dollars for expedited shipping. I lightly scolded my child for waiting until the last minute, a habit that was becoming more routine with a busy schedule. Two days later, I got an e-mail from Amazon that said shipping had been delayed for another two days.

When my child texted me from school a few minutes later, asking if the book had arrived, I cringed as I typed *No*. A split second later, the response came: *Can you get another copy today? I need it. Please?* I replied: *Lack of planning on your part doesn't make an emergency on my part.*

Sometimes the best way to help our kids is to not help them. They often become resourceful and responsible when we simply let them.

These are the moments that are hard for us as parents. At that moment, I was walking into a meeting, and later that evening I would be attending the small group Terrell leads. There was no way I could make it to the closest bookstore in time. I encouraged my child to talk with the teacher and deal with the consequences of getting behind on the project. Plus, I knew this was an important lesson to learn.

I wanted to fix this problem. I didn't want my child to fail. But in my heart I knew that I would be encouraging this pattern to continue if I rushed to make everything okay. So I didn't.

I was relieved when my child called around and was able to find a friend with an extra copy. We both knew it was a stroke of luck. But watching my child develop problem-solving skills was rewarding, and a valuable lesson was learned in the process.

Sometimes the best way to help our kids is to not help them. They often become resourceful and responsible when we simply let them. We can do this by stepping back and being quiet. That doesn't mean we aren't compassionate and caring. It just means we don't jump to fix their problems just because we have the time, money, or resources. Yes, part of parenting is coming to their aid, but if we always rush to do so, we fail to teach them the other part that is just as important as knowing we will be there to help them. And that's letting them know we will be there when we can't help them.

When my kids fail, it hurts me too. But it's a good opportunity to remind them that God teaches us in life's failures and successes. When we follow through in this area, we will often discover the thing we are trying most to teach them (perhaps responsibility or consequences) is learned when we first let them feel the sting of failure.

We Don't Want Them to Feel Left Out

One night as I tucked Emerson into bed and pulled her cozy pink comforter up to her chin, she said, "Mommy?"

"Yes, honey?" I waited.

"I am sad."

"Really, why?" I asked, trying to remember what might have prompted this statement.

"I'm sad I don't have my own iTouch like my friends. A lot of my friends have them and iPhones, too," she said as she rattled off the names of half of the students in her first grade class.

"Why do you want one?" I asked, even though I could have guessed her answer.

"Because my friends have one."

I explained that in our family we decided this wasn't appropriate for her at seven years old. But this wasn't about technology (although—really?—she could have asked for a purple pony named Lucy or a giant stuffed marshmallow that all the kids *must have now*). The point is, we cannot give our kids stuff just because their friends have it. And we cannot give in to giving our kids stuff because our friends are giving it to their kids. *It's a dangerous cycle that is hard to break.* We cannot make our parenting choices based on what others are doing. We have to purpose our lives with intention or we will end up being just like everyone else, caught in a trap in our culture that demands we fit in.

When we parent with intention and moderation, and our kids end up getting something they really want or have worked for, it will be appreciated.

We Don't Want Them to Be Unhappy

A friend sent me a Jamba Juice gift card, and it lay on the kitchen counter for weeks because I thought it would be a fun after-school treat one day. Every time my kids saw it sitting there, they asked if we could go.

We finally had a brief break in our busy lives and piled into the car after dinner for a quick trip. But from the moment we buckled our seat belts, the arguing started. My kids love each other, but "liking" one another seems optional some days. The bickering quickly escalated, and I threatened them from the front seat: *"Stop or we're turning around."*

They ignored my warning and continued picking on and pestering each other. A mile or so later, I sighed and gave my husband a questioning look. He shook his head *no*, and I knew we were about to have some unhappy kids.

Kids' temporary unhappiness—learning to submit to authority and obedience—is worth it if it produces future adults who love God and others.

You know that feeling you get when you're about to knowingly make your kids mad? I hate that. But I'm compelled to do it anyway. Like that time I told my daughter we were done with Disney Channel sitcoms and all the characters' sassy back talk and bad attitudes. I flipped off the TV, and for the next thirty minutes, I felt like I was in the midst of the apocalypse as she cried, stomped her feet, and threw herself across my bed. I encouraged her to get it all out because I wasn't changing my mind. She wailed and whined and then, in true Disney fashion, *let it go.*

I actually love seeing my children happy; I don't set out to make them unhappy. But my husband and I are the authority in their lives. It's our job to place rules and guidelines in our home. It's also our job to follow through with consequences when they are broken. One is a lot easier than the other. So unhappiness happens in our family nearly every day in some way.

And yet their temporary unhappiness as kids—learning to submit to authority and obedience—is worth it if it produces future adults who love God and others. Deep down our kids long for authority and structure. They crave guidelines and rules because that's one of the major ways they feel loved by us. Letting them experience small disappointments now helps them handle big ones later on.

But that doesn't make it easy. As a matter of fact, the tension of doing what's best for our kids even when it means they will be temporarily unhappy is just plain hard. I wrestle with it constantly. The temptation to fix all their problems, ease all their anxiety, give them everything they want, and make life easier is real. But when we do just that, we actually make life in the future a lot harder.

I think we end up buying more stuff because we are trying to purchase happiness or even love, and the excess comes from continually trying to purchase what can't be bought.

Authors Elizabeth Dunn and Michael Norton want us to consider the concept that "underindulgence—indulging a little less than you usually do—holds one key to getting more happiness for your money."[4]

Forbes contributor Robert Glatter finds the ideas expressed by Dunn and Norton revolutionary.

> The concept is that . . . denying yourself the excess that you may ultimately desire may allow you to savor and appreciate the finer things in life. . . .
>
> A more extreme but scientifically proven means of increasing the happiness you derive from your money is a bit more radical—not spending it on yourself. It turns out that people who spend money on others rather than themselves are actually happier in the long run. They derive a greater feeling of

reward and satisfaction and this helps to enrich their inner feelings of sharing and contentment.

So instead of buying that extra watch or TV the next time you have some new found money, consider the alternative: indulging less and offering others the opportunity to share in your wealth.[5]

Underindulgence has led to great joy for our family. From shopping for Christmas presents for a single mom's kids (and dropping them off anonymously on her front porch, waiting and watching from a dark car to see the joy on their faces when they discover the surprise) to giving up a few lazy summer days to counting beads from around the world for a fair trade project at Mercy House. Simply put, we have discovered deep satisfaction in serving and loving people other than ourselves.

It leaves me considering this thought by author and therapist Lori Gottlieb: "Could it be that by protecting our kids from unhappiness as children, we're depriving them of happiness as adults?"[6]

Our excursion to Jamba Juice ended midtrip. Terrell turned the truck around and we headed back home. It took a minute, but the arguing died down, and it got very quiet in the backseat. Then there was a little begging, some promises, and a lot of regret, but we stuck with our decision.

The beauty of parenting is the grace of second chances. That Jamba Juice gift card eventually got used a couple of weeks later and was appreciated even more.

We live in a culture that is obsessed with not only making

our kids happy by giving them everything they want, but also trying to keep them happy. It's an impossible, exhausting task. I've tried it. Maybe you have too. But instead of making kids happier, it just makes them want more. And more often leads to more emptiness. Lori Gottlieb observes how this thinking skews expectations and causes discontent. "It's not enough to be happy—if you can be even happier. The American Dream and the pursuit of happiness have morphed from a quest for general contentment to the idea that you must be happy at all times and in every way."[7]

I think this requirement of being happy all the time is where entitlement thrives. In my parenting poll, when I asked, "What do you want most for your kids?" there were two main answers: I want them to follow Christ, and I want them to be happy. Sometimes both aren't possible at the same time.

Think about it. If we fix every problem, cater to every need, and bend over backwards to keep our kids happy all the time, we are setting them up for a false reality because life won't always offer them the same courtesy. Sometimes professors won't accept excuses, bosses won't make allowances, and banks won't give second chances.

When Emerson was finishing up her second grade year, she asked if I would attend her awards ceremony the last week of school. Her public elementary school, like most across America, makes sure every child receives an award at these events. Personally, I think we do our kids a great disservice when we award them for simply showing up. These participation awards are so common that they don't mean as much to the children as we might think they do. I've witnessed my kids' disappointment in other settings when they didn't receive an award. I've also seen how it inspires them to work harder, and it makes the awards they do get that much sweeter.

I told Emerson I would be there. Her next question caught me off guard.

"Will you bring me flowers?" she asked.

"Honey, what for?" I asked in surprise.

"Because I did a good job? And other parents might give them to their kids," she said a little more hesitantly.

"First of all, we don't ask for people to give us flowers. Second, no," I said firmly. "We will save flowers for graduation or a really special occasion."

Everyone loves getting flowers, and she was asking because she'd seen others receive them, but I knew this was one area I couldn't make her happy in.

Psychologist Wendy Mogel responded strongly after hearing of a soccer coach who said he didn't want his young players to feel "bad" or "devastated" if they lost by too big a margin. "Please let them be devastated at age six and not have their first devastation be in college! Please, please, please let them be devastated many times on the soccer field!"[8]

Jen Wilkin lists four risks she sees when we overindulge our kids:

> We gamble on the future.
> We feed low self-esteem.
> We act neither alien nor strange. [See 1 Peter 2:11-12.]
> We crush contentment.[9]

I am not a gambler, so why would I take those risks? When we give our kids everything they want or bend the rules to make them happy, we are failing to train them to face the ups and downs of life. We can't predict or promise what their economic or emotional lives will hold. It may be that they will face hardship, as most people do. "Compassionate parents raise their children to be prepared for an uncertain future. Raising children who feel entitled to suburban affluence is neither compassionate nor wise."[10]

Our kids don't need more stuff or more freedom; they just need more of us.

Research proves there's a direct link between low self-esteem and materialism. We give our kids more because we think it will make us all feel better, but it actually places a higher value on things than on relationships. And often our kids don't need more stuff or more freedom; they just need more of us.

I don't know about you, but personally I don't want to be the one who doesn't fit in. I think this is the issue that is hardest to accept. We want to fit in, we want our kids to fit in, and we are wrong for both. According to 1 Peter 2:11-12, we should look and be different from the world. "Dear friends, I urge you, as foreigners and exiles, to abstain from sinful desires, which wage war against your soul. Live such good lives among the pagans that, though they accuse you of doing wrong, they may see your good deeds and glorify God on the day he visits us." Our unsatisfied thirst for more makes us materialistic, which only feeds our desire to be like everyone else.

It's hard to be content when we constantly try to keep up with the latest trends and must-haves. When we work to keep up, we are teaching our kids to look and wait for what's coming next, and this tends to make us discontent with what we have right now.

When we overindulge our kids in these areas, we harm them more than help them. It takes courage and consistency to delay good things now for better things later.

GOING AGAINST THE FLOW

Parents

Let's face it: Kids wanting what others have is a part of growing up. It's normal. But that doesn't mean we give in for that reason alone. Here are some ways we can teach truth to our kids.

> Create a family mission statement and hang it on the wall or write it on a chalkboard.
> Put a plan in place. We have to plan for what we say yes to. Be intentional with your time and money. Talk to your kids about things you're saving for or working toward. Let them know that your family wants to stand out as being different and sometimes that means you will need to say no. Explain that sticking to the plan helps protect you from the pressure of buying into the latest fad or must-have, which will be quickly replaced by something else.

Toddlers/Preschoolers

> Start young and limit gifts and the gimmes. Many people do three gifts at Christmas (ask extended family to help you honor this).

> Make cookies together. You may eat one for your
effort, and then give the rest away to brighten
someone's day. Teach your children that we don't
have to keep everything for ourselves.

Elementary

> Clean out closets and drawers, and instead of giving
away only things that they won't miss, urge your kids
to include something they really love to share with
someone else.

> Ask your kids what cause they want to help and then
work together to raise money (through a family garage
sale, a bake sale, or some other method). If you leave it
up to them to live less excessively, they may not, but if
you expose them to people with less and then give them
an opportunity to do something, they will usually join in.

Tweens/Teens

> Add some perspective: Not everyone has (fill in the
blank). It may seem to your son or daughter as if she's
the only one in her class or he's the only one in his
grade or on this planet who isn't fitting in or keeping
up. But if we are going to compare ourselves to others,
let's also compare ourselves to kids who live in poverty.

> Tell your kids that you are more concerned about who
you—and they—are than what you have. I love seeing
my kids happy. But keeping them happy all the time
isn't my number one priority. Parenting is a marathon,
and we have to remember our long-term goal of
raising beautiful people who love God and others.

CHAPTER 4

THE SELFIE SOCIETY

WHEN MY SON WAS A PRESCHOOLER, we enrolled him in Little Tikes soccer at the YMCA. Because that's what you do with boys, right? We wanted to develop his athletic skills, so we decorated him from head to toe in jersey, shin guards, and cleats. The only problem was that he preferred picking daisies in the field with his teammate Grace instead of keeping the ball in play. No matter how hard we coached from the sidelines, he just wasn't into it.

We tried other six-week sports options, and every time, after a few games, Jon-Avery would ask the same question: "Dad, am I the best?" "Mom, I'm the best, right?" He wasn't the best; he was average. We would dodge the truth and ask him, "Are you doing your best?" Because that's what matters. We consistently told him, "It's okay to just be okay."

But like your children and mine, he's growing up in a culture that says you have to be the best at something. Nobody wants average anymore. If parents buy into that mind-set, we end up lying to our kids. Seriously, look at *American Idol.* Some of the contestants were encouraged by family and friends that they could sing. Am I right? And instead of being crowned an idol, they ended up on a blooper reel in everyone's living room.

Years later, Jon-Avery discovered archery, and at some tournaments, he is the best. At others, he's average. But he keeps at it not so that he can become the best, but because he loves it.

One of my favorite Disney movies is *The Incredibles.* I love the story line revolving around a colorful family of superheroes who are living undercover as civilians. Not only does it make me laugh but it also makes me think. In my opinion, this conversation between mother Helen Parr and her oldest son, Dash, is profound:

> *Helen:* Dash . . . this is the third time this year you've been sent to the office. We need to find a better outlet. A more . . . constructive outlet.
> *Dash:* Maybe I could, if you'd let me go out for sports.
> *Helen:* Honey, you know why we can't do that.
> *Dash:* But I promise I'll slow up. I'll only be the best by a tiny bit. [In case you haven't seen the movie, you probably have deduced that Dash's superpower involves speed.]

Helen: Dashiell Robert Parr, you are an incredibly competitive boy and a bit of a show-off. The last thing you need is temptation.

Dash: You always say "Do your best," but you don't really mean it. Why can't I do the best that I can do?

Helen: Right now, honey, the world just wants us to fit in, and to fit in, we gotta be like everyone else.

Dash: But Dad always said our powers were nothing to be ashamed of, our powers made us special.

Helen: Everyone's special, Dash.

Dash [muttering]: Which is another way of saying no one is.

Everyone is special. Everyone is the best at something. We've heard it our entire lives; we've said it and believed it. As Christians, we memorize and teach our children verses such as Luke 12:7, "Indeed, the very hairs of your head are all numbered. Don't be afraid; you are worth more than many sparrows." Every life matters to God, and He has a unique plan for each of us. It's an absolute truth.

But does that make us more special than the next person?

> *We do a great injustice to our kids when we don't allow them to discover their uniqueness through being average.*

Does it make us better? A little cartoon character's conclusion rings true that if everyone is special, then actually no one is. We *are* all special and unique, but the world doesn't revolve around us. And we do a great injustice to our kids when we don't allow them to discover their uniqueness through being average. Camp director Steve Baskin says,

The self-esteem movement has done an entire
generation a deep disservice. It started with the best
intentions. In 1969, Nathaniel Brandon wrote a
paper entitled "The Psychology of Self-Esteem" that
suggested that "feelings of self-esteem were the key
to success in life." Hearing this, many people started
to find ways to confer confidence upon our children.
This resulted in competitions where everyone gets
a trophy and no one actually wins. "New games"
attempted to engage children without any winners
or losers.[1]

The word *special* means, "better, greater, or otherwise
different from what is usual."[2] But when an entire culture
of individuals believes they are better and greater than the
norm, we become a selfie society.

Thanks to all forms of social media, taking "selfies" anywhere, anytime seems to have been around forever, when in
reality the term *selfie* is relatively new. The *Oxford English
Dictionary* declared it to be "Word of the Year 2013"[3] and
added the term as a new entry, saying it is a "pouty self-portrait
typically taken with a smartphone."[4] *The Economic Times* has
said that the selfie has grown from a mere word to a world phenomenon.[5] The market has been bombarded by new technology from phones, cameras, apps, and extendable poles to take
a group selfie, and their sole purpose is to make selfie-taking
easier and more convenient. TV personality Kim Kardashian
made selfies one of her signature social media trends and
has compiled her favorites in a book aptly titled *Selfish*; in
December 2013, two years before the anticipated *Star Wars:*

Episode VII movie hit theaters, the buzz started with a *Star Wars* Instagram account featuring a Darth Vader selfie.[6]

Techinfographics created an infographic dedicated to all things selfie that says a lot about this viral phenomenon. What grabbed my attention was the number taken each day (a million) and how many people are altering or enhancing their photos (36 percent).[7]

While "duck faces"[8] seem harmless, when we look past the image on the camera, we see individuals projecting themselves as the main characters in every story. Self-portraits have been a favorite subject of artists, including Leonardo da Vinci, Rembrandt, and Vincent van Gogh, to name a few, but something seems amiss when our sole purpose for our self-portrait is to share it on social media to invoke an emotion or seek approval from those following our story. I agree with writer Kate Knibbs in *Digital Trends*:

> Taking pictures of yourself all the time is a really weird, self-interested thing to do. Especially if you put them on the Internet and expect feedback. It's asking people to validate how your face looks, not who you are as a person or anything beyond how well you can put yourself together for an "impromptu" snapshot. Doing this a little bit is fine, but making it your main activity on social media is bizarrely solipsistic. . . . Endorsing a culture of selfies will bring us nothing good.[9]

GREAT EXPECTATIONS

Both of my girls have loved American Girl dolls, and each has saved her money to purchase her favorite one. Our youngest, Emerson, is now the same age Madison was when she fell in love with history and dolls. But something has changed. The American Girl doll company has retired nearly all of their traditional historically themed dolls. We've gone from dolls like Kirsten, whose pioneer story included cholera, rough living conditions, and hardships, to Girl of the Year dolls like McKenna, whose biggest challenge is failing grades, a gymnastics injury, and self-doubt. Or you can buy the popular "look-alike" dolls, a mini version of your daughter that she can weave her own story around.

Paul Harvey, a University of New Hampshire professor, says in his research that Generation Y[10] has "unrealistic expectations and a strong resistance toward accepting negative feedback" and "an inflated view of oneself."

He points out,

> A great source of frustration for people with a strong sense of entitlement is unmet expectations. They often feel entitled to a level of respect and rewards that aren't in line with their actual ability and effort levels.[11]

I have seen this to some degree with my kids when it comes to chores and allowance. Several months ago, after a Saturday of cleaning, I walked into the "clean" bathroom to find trash in the wastebasket and a still-dirty mirror. When I asked the one responsible for that chore, the response was, "Mom, you're just a perfectionist." I pointed out the areas that still needed attention and said, "If you were my employee, I wouldn't pay you. You have to do a good job in order to get good pay." I think it's important to teach our kids that the effort they give is related to the outcome they receive.

On the flip side, of course, Generation Y is probably also the most tech savvy and confident of any generation, which can be a great asset to a company.[12]

This is a delicate balance. When we allow selfishness in our culture to invade our homes and impact how we parent, we risk running a child-centered home.

A few years ago, I realized I was guilty of just that—I spent a lot of time centering my days on my kids. It didn't take long for my kids to expect every weekend, every meal at a restaurant, every family moment to not only be kid friendly, but to revolve around them.

Summer was especially that way. One hot June day, an hour after Emerson got home from vacation Bible school, she started complaining that she was bored. One hour after water games! Snow cones! A slimy craft! Dancing and singing! The Best Day Ever!

We were in the *second week* of summer. The second week of sleeping in and already she was slipping and sliding *toward boredom*. Walking around the house, whining about having nothing to do, kicking her foot, and waiting outside the bathroom door. (I wasn't hiding. Really.)

Go. Find. Something. To. Do.

I cracked open the door, and as soon as I saw her empty stare, I realized she was waiting on me to tell her what to do or to do something with or for her. Yes, we had plenty of things coming up in the summer; the calendar was filled with camps and classes, lessons and events. But at that moment, it was just a ho-hum day. Was a little gratitude on her part too much to ask?

Honestly, I couldn't really blame her because for a long time, I was guilty of providing something for every leisure moment of my kids. I bought into this lie that it's my job to make my kids' childhood magical and fun, to guarantee them that every day will be an adventure all about them.

> *I bought into the lie that it's my job to make my kids' childhood magical and fun, to guarantee that every day will be an adventure all about them.*

Our children need to be bored. They need to kick their feet and wait outside of bathroom doors, unanswered. They need to be sent outside or to their rooms to play. They need to turn over the bag of tricks and find it empty.

Because that's when they will discover they don't need stuff to fill their time. They don't need a plan for entertainment. They can create their own.

And when they do, that's when summer turns magical.

I pulled my little one aside, got down on her eye level, and said, "Let me explain summer to you, honey. There will be fun days! We will check boxes off your summer bucket list. We will play. We will work. We will serve. We will have great times. But there will also be a lot of unplanned days; there will be empty hours. There will be days when you've watched enough TV or we won't be leaving the house for something super fun.

"At first, these days may seem boring or like there is nothing to do. And that's okay. Because after you whine and perhaps cry, you will have to make up your own fun.

You'll pick up that book from the library you started. You'll draw doll furniture and cut it out and give your paper dolls a home makeover. You will figure something out. I love to see you having fun, but I will not—I cannot—make every day fun. It's not my job to make every moment the best one of your life. But it is my job to teach you that the days that aren't fun usually end up being the best ones of summer."

Sometimes we have to wait for our kids to remember just how fun having nothing to do can be.

She ended up stomping off, but I found her later with a bucket of Legos where she spent a couple of hours on her own creating the coolest flying space car ever. Sometimes we have to wait for our kids to remember just how fun having nothing to do can be.

We've been known to turn dinner cleanup time into family bonding, also known as arguing over who is doing more than his or her fair share of work. Ah, children. I would usually sigh and just send them all out of the kitchen because it's easier to clean up alone in silence than in a group of discontentment. But then Terrell discovered the key: music. It's easier to "Shake It Off" with loud dancing music. It's not always a party in the kitchen, but the potential is there.

EFFECTS OF A CHILD-CENTERED HOME

I don't think parents start off with the intent of allowing their homes to become child-centered. I know I didn't. It's an easy cycle to fall into but it's much harder to get out of. I didn't want to give up eating out after church on Sunday when my kids were little, so we went to kid-friendly places.

As the kids got older, they didn't want me to keep picking the restaurants. When Terrell and I would choose something they didn't like, there was always complaining. It became easier just to give in to their demands.

From my own experience, I've realized a child-centered home could have more harmful results than helpful ones for our kids in the long run. Here are seven potential problems:

1. *In a child-centered home, kids expect more of us and less of themselves.*
When we create a world that revolves around our kids, it gives them a false security that the bigger world is all about them too. We can fix all their problems and give in to their demands, but the world won't necessarily do them this favor. Sooner or later— in school or at a first job—they will discover life isn't always fair, and they will face sticky situations on their own. I don't think they'll have time to phone home for the solution. In fact,

> Wendy Mogel suggests that children insulated from unpleasant situations or challenges become less capable to deal with adversity. She notes that college deans are seeing a growth in incoming "teacups": students so overprotected by their parents that [they] are effectively incapable of functioning in the new (and parentless) world of higher education. They encounter adversity and "chip like a teacup."[13]

I know a mom who periodically would stay up all night redoing her high school son's school projects because she saw his grades as a poor reflection on herself. But her son continued to do a bad job because he knew his mom would bail him out. I worry about him when he goes to college or lives on his own. Giving our kids this false sense of security that the world will treat them the same is unfair.

2. *A child-centered home puts a strain on your marriage.*
Nothing adds an unnecessary burden to marriage like allowing our homes to be centered on our kids. Yes, there are seasons with newborns and sick babies or circumstances beyond our control when our kids need to come first. But nothing drives a wedge between spouses more than letting your marriage become child-centered. (Later in this book, I will talk about creating a Jesus-centered home. I believe He wants to be the core of our homes and marriages. But for this point, a couple-centered marriage is healthier than a child-centered one.)

As noted in James Sheridan's Marriage Done Right newspaper column,

> Children can strengthen a marriage and bring great satisfaction, but only if couples don't allow their children to become the center of the marriage. . . . A "child-centered marriage" weakens the marriage, and a weak marriage eventually undermines the child. . . . Children need time, lots of it. But they also need a sense of security. And that means maintaining a healthy marriage. . . . [Researcher Shirley] Glass notes, "If you really love your kids, the best gift you can give them is your own happy marriage."[14]

3. *A child-centered home reinforces selfishness.*

Kids don't need to be taught selfishness. "Mine" is usually one of the first words they learn. Remember my daughter's bout with boredom that I mentioned earlier? One busy day a couple of months ago, I held up my index finger when my youngest opened my bedroom door and started to ask me something, reminding her I was on an important business call and didn't want to be interrupted. But she ignored my attempt to quiet her and asked the question loudly, as if my visible warning meant nothing.

I pointed again, more forcefully. My seven-year-old kept right on talking. Even my most threatening face didn't stop her. *This must be really important,* I thought.

"Excuse me for a moment," I said to the person I had called, covered the mouthpiece with my hand, and whispered to my daughter through gritted teeth, "WHAT IS IT?"

She took a tiny step backward and said, "I don't know what to do."

Y'all, I thought my head might spin around.

"Go play. Give me five more minutes," I said, seething.

"But Mom. I need you to tell me what to do."

I finished up the rest of my phone call inside the master bathroom, behind a locked door. When I hung up a few minutes later, I kept thinking about my daughter's words. *I need you to tell me what to do.* When we stop everything we are doing to meet the demands of our kids, we aren't really helping them. We are reinforcing their natural bent towards selfishness. We are telling them that what they want is most important.

We started our shift to a Jesus-centered home years ago,

but we still struggle with the fallout from all the years we let our kids have their way all the time. Please understand me, friends. Our children haven't become less important to us. Terrell and I haven't stopped loving them unconditionally or stopped meeting their needs. We refocused and prioritized our lives for the good of all, not just for one individual, and that has only increased our love for them.

Listen, all humans are naturally self-centered. We want what we want. Our kids are no different. Kids who always get what they want seem happy until they don't get what they want. And then *watch out*. We *can* say no. We *should* say no. It's not easy, but sometimes it's best.

4. *A child-centered home burdens kids with unnecessary pressure.*
When we cater to every need and whim, it weighs down our children with an unhealthy responsibility and burden that they weren't meant to carry, emotionally and mentally. I believe kids want restrictions and guidelines. When we don't provide these, we are setting them up for failure. We can work hard to alter their world so that it's perfect for them all the time, but we aren't with them all the time. Eventually, they will experience life outside the protective bubble.

A percussion teacher at my son's school told me that Jon-Avery was struggling with confidence in a one-on-one rehearsal time. When Jon-Avery messed up a piece of music, he didn't continue on and finish—he would start over. "I think if something doesn't change," the teacher said, "Jon-Avery will be shattered if he doesn't succeed."

"Actually, he might be disappointed or discouraged," I replied respectfully, "but he won't be shattered. When it comes to success, the only pressure he has is what he sets for himself." We can't force our kids to set the bar higher than what they're comfortable with.

Terrell saw evidence of this when he was in middle school, and this story stuck with him. He relates,

> One of my sister's friends didn't have any rules and her parents were permissive. One night she was over for dinner, and one of us was complaining about having a curfew. She told my sister, "I wish my parents loved me enough to set boundaries like your parents do." My family was shocked when she said this, and it gave us a whole new perspective.

5. *A child-centered home narrows our kids' perspective of the world.*

I started my parenting journey wanting to give my kids the world and everything in it. I think it's natural to want the best for our children, and in our society that often translates to "stuff." Just walk into Babies"R"Us. Who knew you needed so much for such a small person? When Maureen, the director of the nonprofit we partner with in Kenya, was speaking and fund-raising in the United States recently, she visited us. We are always thrilled to see her but this was especially exciting because she was expecting her first baby.

I decided to take her shopping at Target. We walked down the baby aisle, and I said, "Okay, this is a baby bottle brush, and this is called a Bumbo. It's for babies who can't sit up yet." Nearly every item I picked up needed an explanation. It was comical because in her culture, you're pretty much thankful if you can provide the basics—diapers, a blanket, and clothes. That's it. The way we live here is unlike how the majority of the world lives.

One of the best lessons for our family was learning how people live in other parts of the world. Talk about eye-opening! In Kenya, there are no thirty-minute meals or quick runs to the store. Instead it takes hours to cook dry beans over an open fire for a simple meal and about the same time to walk to the store a couple of miles away or sit in gridlocked traffic. I realized this exposure and change of perspective was giving my kids a true snapshot of the world, as well as giving them something to compare their lives to. The "get what I want when I want it" business is not the norm, an important concept for kids to grasp.

> *One of the best lessons for our family was learning how people live in other parts of the world. Talk about eye-opening!*

6. *A child-centered home inhibits awareness of others.*
When we focus all our time and attention on our own needs, it's really hard to see the needs of other people. We all probably know people who lack awareness of others around them. They spend all their time trying to meet their own needs, and they are often oblivious to the needs of others. When we allow our homes to be centered on our kids, we do the same thing.

For many years, our family lived a good, often intentional life inside our four walls. We focused on ourselves—what we needed, what we loved, what we wanted. We spent time together, reading the Bible, playing games, focusing on our little family. I think taking care of your family, dreaming a little, splurging at times is great, but when that's all we do, we are creating a self-awareness void. The best way to fill that empty place is by serving others. It could be finding a way to serve as a family at a local non-profit or taking a meal to a new neighbor or passing out blankets to the homeless. Whenever we do something for others, it's in our nature to see life through a new lens—theirs. It's hard to walk away from someone in need and be the same person you were before you met. Serving others not only changes our perspective, it stirs up gratitude because we have a better view of what we have.

> *When we have everything, we are thankful for nothing. When we have nothing, we are thankful for everything.*

7. A child-centered home perpetuates a lack of self-control.

Perhaps the most dangerous result of a child-centered home is how it undermines personal self-control. Self-control is a learned, valued skill that will be an asset for kids their entire lives. When we foster an unrealistic environment that caters to our kids' whims, we fail to give them a reason to exhibit self-control. Toddlers and preschoolers learn it through discipline and consistency. And we, as adults and parents, need to be not only the teachers but also the examples. Let's face it, this area is probably a struggle for most of us at times. As kids get older, if they haven't had to exercise control over what they want, it can affect many areas of their lives—from overspending to sexual promiscuity.

The very thing most parents long to give their kids— a grateful heart—is destroyed in our attempt to simultaneously give them the world. It's hard to have both because true thankfulness is experienced when we first understand we are missing something. And that's hard to teach when we are trying to give them everything. When we have everything, we are thankful for nothing. When we have nothing, we are thankful for everything.

Sometimes we just need a good dose of reality. Wellesley High School English teacher David McCullough Jr. offered graduating seniors exactly that in his speech to the class of 2012:

> You're not special. You're not exceptional. . . . Yes, you've been pampered, cosseted, doted upon, helmeted, bubble-wrapped. Yes, capable adults with other things to do have held you, kissed you, fed you, wiped your mouth, wiped your bottom, trained you, taught you, tutored you, coached you, listened to you, counseled you, encouraged you, consoled you, and encouraged you again. You've been nudged, cajoled, wheedled, and implored. You've been feted and fawned over and called "sweetie pie." . . . But do not get the idea you're anything special—because you're not. . . . Selflessness is the best thing you can do for yourself.[15]

Yes, the opposite of selfishness is selflessness. Think about Jesus' life here on earth. One of the reasons He came to earth in the way that He did was to give us a great example of servanthood. He exemplified Matthew 23:11-12 with his life. "The greatest among you will be your servant. For those who exalt themselves will be humbled, and those who humble themselves will be exalted." Our kids won't learn this principle in the world. When we follow Christ, we enter an upside-down Kingdom with different standards. It's not about being the best or first; it's about being last, about giving up our lives for others. This is when we truly begin to live.

Dave Stone, author of *How to Raise Selfless Kids in a Self-Centered World*, points out how radical this idea is.

> Being others-oriented is about as countercultural as it gets. Self-centeredness is so prevalent in our world that we don't even recognize it anymore. We are a society of the entitled; we think we deserve whatever we have—and then some.[16]

This is our sin nature, and while it may seem natural, it's not beneficial. Dave goes on, "I love the way my friend Nicole says it: 'Society screams *me*, and Jesus screams *them*.' . . . Becoming others-oriented is not a matter of flipping a switch; it's a lifestyle you cultivate."[17]

SELFLESSNESS BEGINS AT HOME

Whenever we have company at our house, we usually double the kids up in rooms so our guests can have a private place to sleep. This has been a challenge for our teenager Madison because it means she has to "really" clean her room. When new friends who were visiting our town for cancer treatments asked for suggestions on where to stay, Terrell and I offered our home. I was hesitant to ask Madison to give up her room, but she had already decided to do so.

Heather and Rian, who are parents of five kids, have

stayed with us many times, and Madison always jumps to offer her bedroom. Thankfully, Heather only needs to come for quarterly follow-up visits. I have been so proud of my daughter's selflessness. And I think that it is having an effect on her too. She told me one day, "Mom, it makes me feel good, like I'm helping them."

If we really want to raise grateful kids, promoting selflessness is a great place to start. It's not necessary to fly across the ocean and volunteer in a third-world country to be selfless. We can start right in our own homes, serving each other. Whether it's taking turns cleaning up dinner dishes or bathrooms, there are countless opportunities right under our noses. In the coming chapters, we are going to dig deeper into cultivating a lifestyle of gratitude so that God will be glorified in our lives and homes.

GOING AGAINST THE FLOW

Parents

Here are some ways to strengthen your marriage:

> Make your spouse a priority.
> Get alone (and lock your door).
> Schedule regular date nights.
> Be affectionate with each other in front of the kids.

Toddlers/Preschoolers

> Resist the urge to tell your kids they are special. Instead say, "God made you unique. There's no one else like you."

> Let your kids be bored every once in a while. It's a healthy exercise to spark creativity.
> Be sure to praise your young ones when you notice them serving in any way.

Elementary
> Have a family meeting and establish boundaries if you're struggling with a child-centered home.
> Create a chore routine. We play "chore roulette" by picking two written chores each out of a jar once a week when we clean the whole house. It's a great way to share the workload.
> Look for opportunities to serve outside your home—make cookies for neighbors, rake someone's yard, clean up trash at the park.

Tweens/Teens
> Challenge your teen to turn the phone around and take pictures of others instead of selfies. Start a conversation about being others-centered. Encourage your teen to think of who that "other" person might be.
> Show them the needs of others rather than telling them. Visit a homeless shelter or a cancer ward together.

CHAPTER 5

MAKING SMART CHOICES ABOUT TECHNOLOGY

"MOM, CAN I PLEASE have a smartphone?" That's the question I heard most often when Madison, my oldest daughter, was in middle school, which is fifth and sixth grade in our town. Some weeks she would ask daily. There would be a reprieve for a week or two, and then she would start again.

I think she wanted a phone so badly because most of her friends had one. She wanted to keep up, interact on social media, and have more freedom like everyone else. While we knew "everyone else" wasn't exactly accurate, it didn't take long to realize that we were definitely in a minority by saying no.

Technology is a huge part of our culture. It changes constantly, and what once was accessible only at the town library is now available at the tips of our fingers on our phones, and even our watches. I love the Internet. I'm a professional blogger and founded a nonprofit that is mostly funded by people who learned about it online. I'm certainly not waving a banner that says it's all bad. But there is evil mixed in with the good, and when our children are young, they don't always know how to navigate it.

As they get into the tween and teen years, some handle the freedom very well while others begin a lifetime struggle with things they are exposed to at an early age.

I know that it's impossible to filter the entire world for my kids. And I can't do it forever. It's not realistic or even my job. Instead, I have to equip my kids because the Internet is a very powerful tool that requires a certain level of maturity and self-control. In our family, I knew once we opened the door to a smartphone, it wouldn't be long before we opened it to social media and more. I was following my gut every time I said no, but also I had read research that showed how vulnerable middle schoolers are—that kids ages ten to fifteen who text excessively (more than 100 texts per day) are more likely to receive or even send sexually suggestive texts.[1]

> *I have to equip my kids because the Internet is a very powerful tool that requires a certain level of maturity and self-control.*

Each time Madison asked the question, our answer was always the same: "No. We want to wait until you're older." As she got older, the answer was still no, but we set high school as the goal for her and her siblings to get their own phones. I don't think there's a magic age for kids to have phones and engage in social media, and I wouldn't dare suggest the perfect time to start. Facebook says it's thirteen,[2] but we decided that was too early for our family. I know our decision to make our kids wait until high school put us in the minority. But instead of making everything off limits, we recognized the technology age we're raising our kids in, so we set up boundaries and started educating ourselves.

There are plenty of parents who never give their kids a phone or laptop, or allow social media accounts, and that's great too. The bottom line is, we have to decide what's best for our family, and if we choose to allow access, we can't parent passively. It requires our involvement.

I jotted down some examples of the differences between active and passive parenting. I'm sure that you could add to the list.

ACTIVE PARENTING	PASSIVE PARENTING
Providing specific guidelines regarding our expectations and limitations	Allowing kids to decide what they want to do and when to do it
Giving our kids what they need (even if it's what they don't want)	Giving kids what they want because they want it
Saying yes or no based on intentional parenting decisions made before a heated or pressured moment	Saying yes or no based on the pressure or emotion of the moment
Leading your family with purpose	Letting the culture lead your family by what's popular

Even though my answer never wavered when my daughter was in middle school and junior high, some days my resolve did. There was a big part of me that wanted to give Madison what she wanted. One of my friends at the time scolded me over coffee one night for making my daughter's junior high life more difficult by not helping her fit in with a phone. I defended my reasoning. Madison wasn't the only one facing pressure, but I knew in my heart that Terrell and I were making the right choice for our child. When it comes to technology, that's exactly what it boils down to. We need to educate ourselves, make a prayerful decision that's right for our kids, and stick to it. Because once we allow access, it's much harder to reverse our decision.

PEER PRESSURE

When Madison started eighth grade, during the first week her public school showed a video to the students in her homeroom class about the dangers of the Internet. Afterward, the teacher asked everyone to raise their hands to signify what kind of device and social media account the students had. Facebook: half the hands were raised. Twitter: a few more. Instagram: the remainder. Madison said she looked around the classroom and was the only one who hadn't raised her hand—for anything.

But instead of feeling embarrassed and left out, she told me later, she felt proud. After watching the video about social media pressure, cyberbullying, and sexting resulting in child pornography charges for some students in the video, she was relieved she didn't have to worry about any of that.

With the Internet in our pocket in this selfie society and pornography a $12 billion industry in the United States and more than $97 billion worldwide,[3] kids are making sexting a part of daily life. According to a poll taken by *The Telegraph* in the UK, 46 percent of teens said that sending naked photos or videos is a part of everyday life for teenagers.[4]

After that day, Madison stopped asking for a phone. She said, "Mom, I don't think I'm ready for a smartphone yet." I marveled at her maturity and wanted to say, "You're a lot more ready than you think." Nearly a year later when she started high school, Terrell and I were thrilled to give her one—with a contract and stipulations, of course. (See Appendix A for the contract we used.)

I can't be passive and assume dangers on the Internet or problems in social media won't touch my children.

Even though Madison is responsible, I still have a love-hate relationship with giving my kids Internet access, whether it's on a phone or the family laptop. It involves work on my part. I can't be passive and assume dangers on the Internet or problems in social media won't touch my children. Some people believe it's cruel to make their kids surrender their phones at night instead of keeping them in their bedrooms and that it's an invasion of privacy to check their child's phone. I am not one of those people.

Here are some of our technology restrictions:

> We get final say in what social media accounts our kids have, and we get to be their "friends" or follow whatever they sign up for.
> We can read our kids' texts if they give us reason to.
> We don't allow FaceTime or other video chatting, chat rooms, etc.

> We won't let our kids interact online with people they don't know, whether it's gaming or followers on Instagram we don't know. Privacy settings on our accounts help control this.

> We require our kids to plug in their technology in the kitchen by nine o'clock every night. Did you know that 87 percent of teens sleep with their cell phones?[5] Not only does this affect their rest, it also becomes an addiction. A blog reader, Erin Frerichs, who is also a teacher, left this comment on my Facebook page about the topic: "I was amazed by the number of parents who said to me at parent/ teacher conferences, 'Well, her/his phone is their alarm clock!' For less than ten dollars at Wal-Mart, you can buy an alarm clock that beeps when it is time to get up; not with every text, Instagram, Snapchat, Facebook alert, e-mail, and Tweet! They need sleep, people!! Solid, uninterrupted sleep!"

> We don't allow apps to be deleted, so we can monitor what's being downloaded.

> We reserve the right to ask our kids to put their phones or media away at any time. After all, they are our phones that we are letting them use. I love what blog reader Kim Adam said: "I pay for it and that makes it MY phone. I am the parent and I will say when and where they can have it."

> We require our kids to pay part of a bill if it is associated with technology.

> We don't allow devices at the dinner table. And please, don't walk and text.

> Ultimately, it is ours and we are letting our child use it. We can and will take technology away if we need to.
> We have a no-media day every week. When we first announced this several years ago, I wish I'd videotaped the response. At the time, it wasn't funny. My kids flipped out—which proved the need for creating media-free hours. It took time and consistency, but they got used to it.

As far as social media and our kids go, we carefully consider each "new thing." We've allowed Instagram and Twitter, which we monitor regularly, and we've changed our minds a time or two. I think there are negatives to each and probably even some positives. I don't think there's a list of right and wrong. But I do think social media access often breeds discontent—and not just in our children. The problem I see with social media is that it creates an alternative world that offers an inflated view. We can easily distort reality and show only the edited or filtered parts of our lives. I've certainly succumbed to unhappiness after a hop into Facebook, so I get it. I'm a middle-aged woman who feels the pressure, and considering that kids are more impressionable and naïve than adults is exactly why we need to be careful and involved.

I have mostly been really proud of my kids' choices, but they are human and we aren't done raising them. I know they will make mistakes and learn from them. We've discovered many teachable moments by getting involved in what they are seeing or saying on the Internet. Although it seemed like we had signed up for plenty of data on Madison's phone, the combination of searching Pinterest, sending out an occasional Tweet, and checking in with friends on Instagram sent her over the number of minutes in her plan. It quickly became an opportunity for a lesson. We explained it cost us an extra $10 and told her if it happened again, she would have to pay it. So when she had another overage a couple of months later, we asked her to cover the cost. She was a little surprised, reminding us that her friends had unlimited data. But she was more careful. She still occasionally goes over her plan, but now she just hands us the money.

Because I don't think this is a cultural phenomenon that will soon be phased out, I offered advice to parents concerning their kids and social media in a blog post on June 21, 2015, based on what I've learned so far. It has been adapted here.

Nothing is ever really private. Statuses and pictures can be shared and altered.

Or permanently deleted. Everything is traceable. I read something really disturbing on Facebook the other day from an old friend, and when I went back to show my husband because I was alarmed, it had been deleted. But it definitely wasn't forgotten.

Some things are better said face-to-face (like apologies or confrontations). Social media makes it easier for us to be cowardly. We need to teach our kids the value of looking someone in the eye and making things right. Sure, it's harder, but they won't forget it.

Remember there are real people with feelings behind every avatar. Lately, I've been on the receiving end of some harsh words. And sometimes I just want to remind the offenders that I'm a real person. I think it's good to teach our kids that our (online) words can hurt.

It's okay to disagree with someone's opinion, but kindness always wins. "If you are not kind on the Internet, then you're not kind." —Glennon Melton. It's as simple as that.

Don't let negative comments to your pictures, statuses, or no likes at all change how you feel about yourself. This one is especially important to teach our girls. There's this whole secret online code between mean girls, and we have to remind our daughters that who they are doesn't change because of how people see them.

It's easier to attain a bad online reputation than a good one—so watch what you say. We've all probably done something online that we regretted. Our words follow us.

Avoid drama. We all read and see things we don't agree with, and I want my kids to use self-control and click off that page.

Don't ever mention your location. Predators don't lure kids at the school bus nearly as much as they do online. Our children need to know the dangers of oversharing.

Take a day of rest from social media. Recently, I asked my teen to take a break from social media. She wasn't in trouble or doing anything wrong. I just noticed she was isolating herself and thought it would be healthy for her to take a couple of days off. Later, she thanked me.

I know so many parents who have handed over an expensive piece of technology without installing parental controls, monitoring usage, or understanding the power they have given their children. And even when we do all those things, there are still risks.

I was talking to my son about it one day when he was using the family laptop in an open area in our office. "Mom, don't you trust us?" he asked, referring to the rule about not taking the computer to their rooms.

"Honey, years ago, you had to type in bad words to find bad things on the Internet. But that's changed. Now these bad things—from spam to pornography to child predators—look for you."

I've talked to many parents who've said it's an invasion of my kids' privacy for me to read their texts or e-mails. I disagree. I think it's important to stipulate with our kids before they are handed a piece of technology that this is a part of the deal. Lynda Gould added this comment to the online conversation: "We had police detectives come to a PTO meeting to speak to parents about protecting our kids on social media and cell phones. They said you should know all your kids' passwords and be checking their text messages daily. In our small town they have busted men pretending to be teens on Facebook, friending kids, getting to know them through conversations, and then asking to meet them. People don't realize how much information can be gathered from their pictures—a school name or mascot, street names, hangouts, etc., so make sure all their settings are private. This is NOT invading their privacy—it is protecting your children."

I recently got an e-mail from a blog reader that made me feel physically sick as I read it. Amy asked me to share her experience because "I want all parents to hear our story and know that in this world today, the smallest things can change our children forever."

In Amy's words:

My eight-year-old has an iPad that was given to her as a gift. I set up the iPad and put rules in place. It is linked to my iPhone so that I am notified if any functions I have turned off get turned on. I hid or turned off the Internet, e-mail, & text messaging. There is a password needed to load any app even if it's free. FaceTime rings to my phone as well as her iPad and it's only allowed with family. She uses it for apps I have approved, and that's really all she has access to. I thought I had all the bases covered.

She asked if she could take her iPad to a sleepover. I asked the mother, and she was fine with it. I should have also asked, "Will they have Internet access?" but I didn't ask that question. It never occurred to me that some younger kids have unlimited, unsupervised access to the Internet. I let my daughter down when I did not ask if there would be Internet access.

My daughter and her friend got on the Internet on her friend's iPad and started searching. They looked at a few videos that my daughter considered harmless to watch. Then the girls decided to search "naked people dating," "naked people kissing," "hot," and "sexy." I am sure you can imagine the images they saw. It was late at night and when the mother came in to tell them it was time for bed, my daughter started to cry, saying they made a bad choice and looked at inappropriate stuff on the iPad. My daughter asked if she could be taken home.

When my daughter was brought home, the friend's mom explained that the girls had looked at inappropriate stuff on the Internet, but she also said that she didn't think it was porn. I tried to be calm as I listened to her, all the while thinking, *Hopefully, it wasn't too bad.* My daughter probably felt like it was unsuitable because what she is permitted to see is limited. I do not allow her to watch certain TV shows that air on the Disney Channel or Nickelodeon because I feel they are inappropriate for her age.

When I talked with my daughter, she said she wanted to start her life over and never see anything like that again. It was her idea to search "naked people dating" and "naked people kissing." The graphic details she gave tipped me off that she did see full porn.

I started asking her questions: "Has anyone searched these topics with you before?" "Have you ever seen anyone date or kiss naked?" "What would make you think to search for that?" "Have you ever seen anything like that on TV?" Through the conversation, most answers were no, then she said, "Well, Mom, the only time I ever saw that was on your TV the other morning. Remember when the news talked about that girl dating naked?"

Then it clicked. The day before, as we were turning off the TVs before we all left for work and school, *Good Morning America* was covering a reality show contestant who was suing the TV show *Dating Naked* for showing too much of her. My other daughter (who is six years old) heard this and said, "What is dating naked? That is gross."

At the time, I glanced at the TV and a clip from the show was on. My eight-year-old asked, "Why would they show her naked?"

"She chose to go on a show and be naked and now she is upset about how the show turned out," I replied quickly. Looking back now, I should have had a longer conversation about that show. The entire scenario was over in ninety seconds before we rushed out the door, went on with our day, and never said another word about it.

Until the next night, when she was obviously still thinking about that story she heard on the news. She had unlimited & unsupervised access to the Internet. She probably thought, *I can find out the answer on my own.* Well, needless to say, their little young eight-year-old minds will never be the same. They had no idea what they would see. I thank God for her honesty and courage to tell an adult what happened. We are now seeking the help of a counselor to make sure we handle this effectively and in a manner that will hopefully help her to not carry guilt and shame forever.

I appreciate Amy's brave warning not just about Internet access, but also concerning media. I think we all know that pornography and explicit images are found easily and often accidentally online, and we set up restrictions and work hard to filter those out. But if we have the TV tuned in to reality shows, the hottest series, or even the news, we might be exposing our children to what we are trying to keep out of our homes. Media is an ever-present danger.

I knew the exact show Amy was referring to in her e-mail because a few weeks earlier we were visiting my in-laws at their rural farm and the show was mentioned on the news. My mother-in-law quickly turned it off, but this type of potentially damaging exposure happens fast, usually when we least expect it.

Think about how much TV has changed in the last few years. What used to be taboo is now prime-time viewing in our living rooms. It's not uncommon to see same-sex couples in relationships, unmarried people in bed together, a lot of cleavage, and even more when there is a wardrobe malfunction at a Super Bowl. We're momentarily outraged that it becomes "news" but eventually let it go.

In 2007, the Barna Group reported that Christian parents are not comfortable with media but we buy it for our kids anyway. According to the study, "the born again Christian population of the US is likely to spend more than $1 billion on media products such as CDs, DVDs, video games, and magazines for children under the age of 18 despite parental misgivings about the moral content or developmental [e]ffects of those resources."[6]

> *Think about how much TV has changed in the last few years. What used to be taboo is now prime-time viewing in our living rooms.*

We have a TV in our family room, but it only plays Netflix with a parental password. The other TV is in our master bedroom. When Emerson was in first grade, we got in the habit of letting her watch the Disney Channel for thirty minutes of downtime after school. It didn't take long before I began to notice that her attitude started getting sassier than usual.

One day it dawned on me that she sounded exactly like one of the tween characters on television. I mentioned it to Terrell, and he said, "We shouldn't even allow her to watch those shows. There's a lot of disrespect of parents." I agreed. We sat her down and told her we had made a mistake by allowing her to watch shows that encouraged disrespecting parents. "We've decided you can't watch these shows any longer." She cried for about ten minutes and then never asked again. Her attitude improved too. Now our TV is rarely on except during NASCAR season or when we tune in to *Duck Dynasty*. Yes, we are rednecks.

TAMING GAMING

Our girls have never been interested in video games the way our son is. From a very early age, we saw the magnetic pull for him to gaming and because of it we immediately restricted his use. We followed game ratings religiously, and if it was rated Teen or Mature, it wasn't allowed. We established gaming rules for our family—that's not to say your rules are wrong if you allow what we don't. But there are ratings for a reason, and we chose not to expose him to the violent fight sequences, foul language, or depictions of scantily clad women.

Without a doubt, this was one of the hardest things for our son regarding peers. When he was in the fourth grade, he was teased and made fun of by several Christian boys (which really made me mad). We would remind him that every family had the right to make their own rules, and we encouraged him to ignore the teasing and worked with him to find different friends. He would tell us that he didn't even want to play the games—he just felt pressured to because his friends were.

Today, as a teenager, he still has the same outdated gaming system with a couple of sporting games. He rarely plays these days; he would much rather beat on his drums or hone his archery skills outdoors.

Going against cultural norms is hard. It makes our kids

feel left out and makes us ache for them. But if we stick to our convictions—whatever they may be—we won't regret it. We aren't against media; we just recognize the dangers and keep it off more than it is on. It's really hard to teach our kids to be different from the world if we look just like it. It's time to take back our living rooms, tune out media, and turn off technology.

The bottom line in our technology-driven culture and media-accessible world is that sooner or later our kids will be exposed to something we don't want them to see. We can exhaust ourselves trying to filter out everything and then a kid with a phone at the library can show our child something he or she shouldn't see. It's happened to us.

> *It's hard to teach our kids to be different from the world if we look just like it. It's time to take back our living rooms, tune out media, and turn off technology.*

THE NECESSITY OF TEACHING SELF-CONTROL

It was the middle of the night, or day, or whatever that fog of time is called when your jet-lagged family is between flights at an airport in Paris, on the other side of the world. We had an extra hour before we boarded, but we had a mission to accomplish—find ChapStick for our windburned lips. We stumbled into one of those airport stores that have everything from duty-free cigarettes to luggage and split up to start our search. My husband walked one way, but I thought I spotted the familiar tubes and headed the other with my little one following behind me. The label was in French and

I wasn't sure if it was the right thing so I turned to hunt for an English-speaking attendant.

That's when I saw my two older kids. My teen daughter had a shocked look on her face and was just turning to look for me. I heard her say her brother's name sharply after she noticed what he was staring at, and his head snapped up just as I walked toward them. "Mom?" he said, looking confused. I scanned the row of magazines in front of him in the center of the store. Pornography.

It was Europe, after all.

"I didn't mean to look," he said. "I just . . ."

"It's okay, Son. Looking once is unavoidable. It's what we do after that first look that matters."

Everything is filtered in our home: We have protected Internet, our Netflix account has a parental password, we opted for additional security on Google images, and we installed Net Nanny on our phones.

Terrell and I aren't paranoid parents; we are proactive. Plus we are highly sensitive to this topic since it nearly destroyed our marriage ten years ago.[7]

We are also prepared. We talk together about the dangers online. We have a stack of books we're working our way through from living in purity to fighting lust. We are open about what our kids are exposed to from peers.

Protecting our children from our sexually charged culture is something we work hard at. And in one unavoidable moment, it happened. My sixth grade son saw pornography right in front of me.

You can't stand in a checkout line at a grocery store and miss Miley Cyrus on the front of a tabloid, hanging nude from a wrecking ball. And really, we're all just one click away from something we can't un-see. The most important thing we can teach our kids is self-control. Because let's face it: No matter how well we parent, our kids are going to be tempted. It goes with being human. Self-control is the ability to control our emotions, abilities, and desires. It's the power to stop spending money we don't have, to tell our kids no when entitlement rears its ugly head. It's exactly what we need to teach our kids to keep them from looking the second time.

Without self-control, we are absolutely defenseless against sin.

Without self-control, we are absolutely defenseless against sin. "A man without self-control is like a city broken into and left without walls" (Proverbs 25:28, ESV). When the word *self-control* is used in the Bible, it describes a person who is willing to get a grip on his life and take control.

Self-control is the key to living in our sex-crazed world without giving in to its lustful appeal. And as hard as it is to accept, our kiddos are sexual creatures and at some point in their lives, it will appeal to them. That's why we can't wait. Here are three things we can do to help our kids (and ourselves) exercise self-control in their lives:

1. *Ask God for it.* Self-control is a gift from God. The more we work on our relationship with Him, the more He empowers us.
2. *Model it.* Our kids are watching us, and we are their example. When you blow it, apologize and try again.
3. *Teach it.* It's easy to feel unprepared. Don't be afraid to rely on solid resources (see Appendix C).

After I paid for the ChapStick, we headed back toward our gate in the airport. My husband pulled our son close as they walked together. "Whenever you see something like that," Terrell said to him, "look away immediately. Bounce your eyes and try really hard not to look again. You might be tempted to look again, but ask God to help you have self-control not to."

I'll never forget that cold December day at the airport—not as a day of failure, but as a day of opportunity to teach my kids the importance of self-control and second chances.

I appreciate Heather Enright's comment on my blog:

> Parenting in this technology age is HARD. We are
> pioneers and it's hard to keep up with the ever-
> changing technology. But I believe if we stick to
> our convictions, then our kids will thank us later.

I love the way she calls us pioneers, don't you? Pioneers blaze a new trail; they learn from their mistakes; they adapt, survive, and thrive in hard conditions. We can do the same. As believers trying to raise Christ-followers, it's a difficult task, but it's not impossible.

GOING AGAINST THE FLOW

Parents

> Establish restrictions and guidelines for technology before you allow it.
> If you haven't done so, it's not too late to go back and

start again. Have a family meeting and explain your rules.

> Make your child's room a media-free zone.
> Be consistent for one month with your rules, and you'll establish a family habit.
> Read *Growing Up Social* by Gary Chapman and Arlene Pellicane, a great resource on this subject.

Toddlers/Preschoolers

> Ninety percent of parents allow kids younger than two years to watch electronic media.[8] This can't be good. Every time you're tempted to hand over your phone to your toddler, pick up a book to read to her instead.
> Keep a "distraction bag" in your purse or car for those moments in public when your child becomes bored and you would normally hand him a device. Suggested distraction bag contents: stickers, Band-Aids, small cars, etc.

Elementary

> Begin the conversation about the dangers of media with your kids. Don't just assume they know what to avoid.
> Before allowing your kids to spend time at their friends' homes, check with the other parents about restricted Internet access.
> Regulate screen time on any electronics—not just as a punishment or consequence, but as a reward.

In summer months, we offer "media minutes" in exchange for "reading minutes."

Tweens/Teens

> Have an open conversation about apps you don't want your kids to install on their devices, the lure of pornography, sexting, etc.
> Monitor their media usage. Some parents might think this is an invasion of privacy. We don't. When our children are allowed access to the Internet, they understand that our agreement means that Terrell and I have the right to oversee it.
> Suggest one media-free day a week and see what the response is.

PART III

RESISTING THE CURRENT

Do not love the world or the things in the world. If anyone

loves the world, the love of the Father is not in him. For all that

is in the world—the desires of the flesh and the desires of the eyes

and pride [in possessions]—is not from the Father but is from the

world. And the world is passing away along with its desires, but

whoever does the will of God abides forever.

I JOHN 2:15-17, ESV

CHAPTER 6

CULTIVATING OBEDIENCE

FAMILY MOVIE NIGHT AT our house is probably more about eating pizza in front of the TV than the actual movie. One Saturday night, we were curled up with blankets, a couple of us on the floor and the rest sharing the couch, enjoying a relaxing night together. Toward the end of the movie, Emerson, a second grader at the time, got up and pulled out a folding chair to sit on. I ignored her until she stopped sitting on the chair and started climbing through it.

"Honey, stop. You're going to get hurt. Watch the movie," I whispered. But she continued.

A couple of minutes later, the chair fell and she nearly closed it on her finger. I said again, "Stop. You're going to hurt yourself." She told me she was fine and shrugged off my warning.

Y'all know where this is going, right?

Two minutes later, she did pinch her finger. Ah, natural consequences. She started crying so I checked for damage. (There wasn't much.)

I didn't feel very sympathetic, but I said, "I'll go get you some ice if that will help."

She said, "Wahhh!"

Terrell paused the movie, and seeing that she would survive, gave a little laugh and said, "Honey, Mom told you to stop." Well, Emerson forgot all about her pinched finger, and her pain turned to anger at our lack of sympathy. In her rage, she crossed a line (the one parents all have) and said things she shouldn't have. We told her to go ahead and get ready for bed.

She wasn't happy about that at all.

Maybe it's just our house, but sometimes it's easier to ignore disobedience. We let our kids act out, blame their behavior on being tired, and look the other way. Sometimes. But once we decide the consequence (in most cases I second-guess myself), we do more harm than good if we back down. Obedience isn't easy, but we make parenting even harder when we don't follow through.

Parenting is one of the most difficult things on the planet, right up there next to marriage. That's why this verse in Ephesians is so important and challenging.

> Children, do what your parents tell you. This is only right. "Honor your father and mother" is the first commandment that has a promise attached to it, namely, "so you will live well and have a long life."
>
> EPHESIANS 6:1-3, MSG

We are all born into disobedience, and sin causes us to focus on ourselves. So asking kids to obey is an unnatural directive. I warned my firstborn when she was a two-year-old to stay away from the stove because it was hot, and she looked me in the eye and replied defiantly, "No!" And then she marched over and touched the stove. Obedience is a learned behavior that places our authority over our kids. Without this authority, there is recklessness.

I didn't have to say, "I told you so"; instead I stuck her burned little finger in ice. Some lessons are learned the hard way.

Obedience is a learned behavior that places our authority over our kids. Without this authority, there is recklessness.

God calls us as parents to teach our kids to obey us. Obedience is expected, not suggested. Before our kids learn to submit to God, they submit to us. In my early parenting years, I made the mistake of expecting immediate obedience all the time, which, when it didn't happen, only left both me and my child frustrated and discouraged. To be honest, as an adult I don't always obey God the first time He expects me to. And yet, as author Sally Clarkson says, that doesn't keep God from extending His grace to us each and every time.

I have made so many mistakes over the years . . . and still [God] is there loving me, instructing me, showing me His compassion and gently leading me daily to better understand His holy and righteous standard for me.[1] . . . He has never pointed out all of my weaknesses and disobedient attitudes at once— and if He did, I would be devastated.[2]

I believe one of the ways children learn submission to God and doing what He says is by being taught to submit to the authority of their parents. So yes, require it, but do so with love and grace because deep down, I think our kids want rules and guidelines and the structure obedience brings.

If we aren't our kids' authority, who is? They are.

My teenage daughter had a school friend over for dinner. I heard Madison tell her friend, "I need to plug in my phone downstairs at nine o'clock. It's one of my parents' rules."

"Really? My parents really don't care." It wasn't her friend's response that made me sad—it was the way she said it with a certain longing.

We aren't just the provider and protector for our kids; we are their authority. We have to expect obedience because God expects us to be in authority. If we aren't our kids' authority, who is? They are. I think kids in our culture lack a healthy fear of their parents. Often they see us only as their protectors and providers. But they need to have a reverent fear of us. They need to know that there is a consequence to disobedience.

One of my kids came home disgusted at a classmate one day. "Mom, this kid wanted the newest phone that just came out, but his parents said no. So do you know what he did? He dropped his phone and broke the screen on purpose so they would have to get him another one." This kid definitely needed a good dose of godly fear of his parents, but instead they played into what he wanted and put him in charge by buying him another phone.

On the night of the home movie incident, as I tucked

Emerson into bed while the movie finished playing, we talked about some of her choices, and she clearly understood why her action caused an early bedtime. As hard as it was, it was also a clear reminder that disobedience leads to discipline. Obedience is not a suggestion; it's a requirement with a consequence. It's hard but it's necessary. We discipline because we love.

In this all-out match against sin, others have suffered far worse than you, to say nothing of what Jesus went through—all that bloodshed! So don't feel sorry for yourselves. Or have you forgotten how good parents treat children, and that God regards you as *his* children?

My dear child, don't shrug off God's discipline,
    but don't be crushed by it either.
It's the child he loves that he disciplines;
    the child he embraces, he also corrects.

God is educating you; that's why you must never drop out. He's treating you as dear children. This trouble you're in isn't punishment; it's *training*, the normal experience of children. Only irresponsible parents leave children to fend for themselves. Would you prefer an irresponsible God? We respect our own parents for training and not spoiling us, so why not embrace God's training so we can truly *live*? While we were children, our parents did what *seemed* best to them. But God is doing what *is* best for us, training us to live God's holy best. At the time, discipline isn't much fun. It always feels like it's going against the grain. Later, of course, it pays off handsomely, for it's the well-trained who find themselves mature in their relationship with God.

HEBREWS 12:4-11, MSG (italics in original)

We are training our children for life, but we have to do so in love and with grace, careful not to crush them with our expectations or discipline. As our kids grow and mature into young adults, they will get glimpses into the *why* of obedience.

A PLACE FOR GRACE

When I was in the tenth grade, I went on one of my first dates with a boy I really liked. My parents had firm rules about dating, one of which was that I wasn't to be alone with a boy at either of our houses. But that's exactly what happened after we left the Valentine's dance early. I knew my parents weren't home, so we went to his house. And before I knew it, I was sitting on his bed while he changed in his closet. We were completely alone in the house. When he kissed me, all I could think about was my parents' rule, and for the first time, I understood the *why* behind it. My disobedience could have put me in a dangerous situation, and considering my racing heart, I was a danger to myself. Thankfully, my date was a really good guy, and we eluded temptation when he agreed to say good night and took me to my house.

I didn't become perfectly obedient after that incident, but

I appreciated my parents' rules and understood they were for my protection and provision.

Ephesians 6:4 tells us, "Fathers, don't exasperate your children by coming down hard on them. Take them by the hand and lead them in the way of the Master" (MSG).

I exasperate my kids when I demand obedience but lack grace in handling their disobedience or failures well.

I know I have exasperated my kids when I demanded obedience but lacked grace in handling their disobedience or failures well.

Tedd Tripp, the author of *Shepherding a Child's Heart*, cuts parents some slack.

> During times of failure . . . , your teens need positive interaction. You need to keep your eye on the goals you have for your children. They need Mom and Dad to be constructive and creative. You need to have a proper sense of proportion, remembering that your child is worth much more than a car [or something else they have wrecked or ruined]. . . . What I have in view is parental interaction that is full of hope and courage. This interaction is able to turn a fiasco into an opportunity to learn and go forward.[3]

There must be a healthy balance in our parenting. We can't offer too much grace and not enough discipline or vice versa. I love this comment from my parenting poll: "Sometimes I feel bad because the follow-through is difficult, consistency is difficult, and requiring it of myself feels like a sacrifice, but when I do say no (in their best interests), usually the lesson is worth learning. Both for them and for me!"

FROM APPRECIATION TO EXPECTATION

For our tenth anniversary, Terrell gave me the best gift: a clean house. He hired a lady to come and clean our home from top to bottom. This was a humbling experience, not only because we invited a stranger to serve our family, but also because it showed just how dirty our house really was. I had no idea. There's nothing like sweeping all your filth into one giant pile to make it evident. I'm a neat freak by nature, but I discovered that neatness doesn't always mean cleanliness.

Terrell had heard James Dobson on a Focus on the Family radio program say that one of the best gifts you could give a mom with young kids was a housecleaner. The idea behind it was that anyone can clean a house, but only a mom can raise her children, and too often moms get frustrated and discouraged about housecleaning and spend most of their energy there. Well, I totally agreed. So we gave up cable TV and a couple of other extras for a season and hired a wonderful woman who needed a job to come twice a month to help clean our home.

Those two days a month quickly became my favorites. For me as a busy mom who worked from home, those acts of service were like a reset button. I understood it was a luxury few families could afford, but right or wrong, I justified it. I was working and volunteering countless hours for our non-profit and felt I deserved it. As the kids grew, they took on age-appropriate chores, and Terrell and I continued to do what was needed, but what once had been a greatly appreciated service became an expectation for all of us. That didn't become apparent until the day I asked my son to pick up his room and he said, "But the maid is coming."

Clearly, it was time to make some changes. I realized having someone serve our family in this way was robbing my now capable children of an opportunity to learn about hard work and serve each other. We were missing a good opportunity to work together to accomplish a necessary task.

Sometimes on the surface, everything looks good, just like my house did. But when you start peeling back the layers (or moving a piece of furniture to clean under it instead of around it), you discover things aren't always what they appear to be. We had gotten lazy, and it was time to clean house—and not just with a vacuum and duster. It was time to sweep up entitlement and expectations.

We thanked the wonderful lady who had served us so well, divided up the household chores, and created a family economic system. (I'll explain more about what works for us in chapter 9.) Within weeks, we were all very aware of the blessing we had taken for granted. I won't lie, there were a lot of complaints and whining, but it was the right decision for us.

CLEANING HOUSE

So how do we walk in obedience to God and also expect it from our kids? How do we swim upstream against the strong current of excess? We do the same thing in our parenting that we do in our home when we recognize we have too much stuff. We clean house and get rid of it.

I'm not a parenting expert (maybe you've gathered that

by now), and my list might look different than yours. Here are some of the areas we decided to clean up.

Handout Mentality

A couple of years ago in December, I got behind with all the holiday busyness, and when I finally had a chance to sit down and wrap a couple of Christmas gifts, it was already late in the season. I don't know about your house, but the minute I do this every year, my kids get really interested in what's happening.

"Mom, when are you taking us shopping to buy gifts for you and Dad?" one of my kids asked.

"Do you have money to buy gifts?" I asked.

"Well, I was thinking you could give us money to, um, buy your gifts," came the answer.

As a part of our family's economic plan, we give our kids money every month if they complete their assigned chores. After they give a percentage into their savings and tithe, we stress that this money can be spent however they want, but we expect them to take care of their own entertainment and gifts for others. When I reminded my daughter of this, she said, "Oh, I wanted to buy a cute Christmas shirt with my money." *Ah, choices.*

> *I refuse to rob my kids of the privilege of hard work [and its monetary rewards] because that's when the joy of giving is revealed.*

When I polled my other two kids, they were also short on funds and big on expectations. Now, I'm not a Scrooge, and I didn't want to rob my kids of the opportunity to give gifts to others. But I also refuse to rob them of the privilege of hard work because that's when the joy of giving is revealed. I hired them for some jobs around the house and yard, and when they shopped and used their own money, it made all the difference.

If we hand out money freely, most kids will take it, and it won't take long for them to acquire the habit of keeping their hands out for more. If we require a little sweat and hard work, we are flipping a switch and beginning to do away with the "you owe me" mentality.

Goody Bag Mentality

My first two kids are barely two years apart. On Madison's fourth birthday, Jon-Avery was nearly two. I didn't want him to feel bad that she was getting gifts and he was not (in other words, I didn't want him to have a tantrum), so I gave him a gift on her birthday. But a couple of months later, she expected one on his birthday. Before long, I realized I had created a monster of a problem and put a stop to it. It's good for kids to learn that they aren't always the center of attention and that it's wonderful to celebrate others.

We've probably all taken our kids to an over-the-top birthday party a time or two. We might have even thrown one for someone we love. We've attended parties where the goody bags we took home were far better than the gift we brought. And while I appreciated the hostesses' generosity, I also felt it was unnecessary, especially in our society where we already have so much.

It's okay for our kids not to be rewarded all the time. Goody bags are harmless, but if the mentality behind giving these party favors is to not make kids feel bad, then maybe we are missing the point. And it's not just birthday parties—it is school parties, holidays, made-up holidays, soccer parties, you name it. We constantly reward our kids with trinkets they don't need and that eventually end up in the garbage. The intent of a caring mom who has the time to make thirty intricate cat cupcakes is certainly admirable, but the message we send our kids every day is about more, more, more—and it doesn't take long for a special treat to become an expected one.

Participation Awards

I can still remember my pudgy three-year-old son's soccer party at the end of the season. Group sports were still very new for our family, and I was surprised when I got an order form to buy my toddler a trophy. It didn't feel genuine, but I certainly didn't want him to be the only one not getting one. I was sucked right into the $3-billion-a-year trophy industry[4] when I paid for his made-up award. He held it high like an Olympian that day while I took a picture, although we all knew he had barely even run down the field at all. It was cute and seemed harmless. He didn't complain when I stopped buying trophies, but it took some time for me to stop feeling guilty when he didn't get one.

Journalist Ashley Merryman addressed the subject in her *New York Times* article "Losing Is Good for You": "Awards can be powerful motivators, but nonstop recognition does not inspire children to succeed. Instead, it can cause them to underachieve."[5] We all probably have a shelf or a shoebox with our kids' participation ribbons and a trophy or two. It has become the standard in our society. But it's affecting our kids in a way that was unintended. Instead of making them want to win, it makes them want to quit if they don't win.

Merryman examines the long-term effects too.

In June [2013], an Oklahoma Little League canceled participation trophies because of a budget shortfall. A furious parent complained to a local reporter, "My children look forward to their trophy as much as playing the game." That's exactly the problem, says Jean Twenge, author of *Generation Me*.

Having studied recent increases in narcissism and entitlement among college students, she warns that when living rooms are filled with participation trophies, it's part of a larger cultural message: to succeed, you just have to show up. In college, those who've grown up receiving endless awards do the requisite work, but don't see the need to do it well. In the office, they still believe that attendance is all it takes to get a promotion.

In life, "you're going to lose more often than you win, even if you're good at something," Ms. Twenge [said]. "You've got to get used to that to keep going."[6]

Constant Praise

I think telling our kids they've done a good job when they have is great. It's the overpraising that comes off as artificial and disingenuous and causes more harm than good. I know I've been guilty of saying, "Good job" and "You're the best!" when their attempt was just average. Kids know the difference.

Stanford University psychology professor Carol Dweck "found that kids respond positively to praise; they enjoy hearing that they're talented, smart and so on. But after such praise of their innate abilities, they collapse at the first experience of difficulty. Demoralized by their failure, they say they'd rather cheat than risk failing again."[7]

I think most of us naturally praise our kids because they like to hear it. But it's more helpful to replace constant praise with encouragement. One definition of the word *praise* suggests that praise glorifies; by comparison, encouragement inspires. I've tried to keep that in mind when I interact with my kids. I was driving home from school one day and Emerson was telling me about a test she had been worried about. When she told me she had done well, I didn't praise the grade—I affirmed her for studying hard. I immediately saw a different expression in her eyes in the rearview mirror, and I could tell she was inspired to do it again. I once heard someone say, "Don't tell you kids, 'I'm proud of you,' tell them, 'You should be proud of yourself.'"

Replace constant praise with encouragement.

Recurring Rescue

It's natural from the beginning of our parenting journey for us to see ourselves as the rescuers and our kids as the rescued. We want to take care of our children. In the beginning, they are helpless and innocent and depend on us for everything. But babies grow, and when they take that first baby step, it is away from us toward independence. It is natural. If they fall, we scoop them up. We make the falls in life better.

When Madison started preschool, she cried hysterically every time I left her. It made me feel terrible. I would stand by the door and whisper encouraging words in her ear; I would offer countless hugs. I would wring my hands and pace and check through the classroom window, only for it to start again if she saw me. When I finally left, it would take me an hour to get over the trauma I had put her through.

One day, a few weeks later, the teacher came out into the hall while I was still there. "The minute you leave her and she knows you're gone, Madison wipes her tears, stops crying, and says, 'Okay, I'm done now.' She's crying for you, not for herself." No wonder that when I'd pick her up from preschool, she would chatter about her day as if she loved every minute of it!

All that time I thought she wanted to be rescued, and instead she just wanted to know I would rescue her if she needed me to. Part of our job is to reassure our kids that we will be there for them, and we are, but the rest of the job requires that we walk away. Kids will continue to let us rescue them if we continue to rush to their side.

When Madison started marching band a few weeks before high school, she would take a big jug filled with ice water with her every day, a necessity in the Texas summer heat. The first day she forgot her jug, she called and I brought it to her, a twenty-minute trip one way. After all, I didn't want her to get dehydrated. The second time she forgot it, I told her to fill up her eight-ounce water bottle at the water fountain, which she did numerous times again that day. I don't know if she ever forgot the water jug again, because I never heard her mention it. I let her solve her own problem.

Most kids will let us continue to solve their problems if we play along. I'm obviously not against helping my kids out. Mistakes happen and we all get busy and forgetful, but when it becomes a habit and we consistently bail our kids out, we are entitling them to continue the pattern. And this mentality has produced a society of adultolescents.

An adultolescent is defined as "a young adult or middle-aged person who has interests, traits, etc., that are usually associated with teenagers."[8] *Newsweek* featured an article on this new breed of overgrown teens in their twenties and even thirties who still live at home or move back after college, citing findings of an online survey that "60 percent of college students reported that they planned to live at home after graduation."[9] These are young adults who depend on their parents for both an allowance and help with landing a career job. The article describes a frightening reality.

> "I've seen parents willing to destroy themselves financially," says financial planner Bill Mahoney of Oxford, Mass. "They're giving their college graduates $20,000, $30,000, even $40,000—money they should be plowing into retirement." And it might only buy them added years of frustration. Psychiatrists say it's tough to convince a parent that self-sufficiency is the one thing they can't give their children.[10]

As hard as it may be, we have to let our kids fail. It's the only way they truly learn how to succeed. It's natural for young children to gain independence and start to move away from us as they learn to walk and run. Self-sufficiency is as natural as those first steps. Don't be afraid to let them take these steps, and when they fall or fail (they will do both), it's okay to let them stand back up by themselves. It starts with saying no and following through, and then backing away and letting them learn how to navigate the world on their own.

We can all probably identify things in our lives we should get rid of, but we also need to have a checklist of things we should add, with grace and obedience at the top of the list.

GOING AGAINST THE FLOW

Parents

> Cleaning house is hard work. Cleaning our temple—our hearts and attitudes—is even harder. At this point, you might be feeling overwhelmed (hopefully inspired, too). Start small. Pick one area that you can start "cleaning." Is it too much media time? A general lack of obedience when you ask your children to do something? We clean house one room at a time and the same goes for getting our family back on track.

> Be consistent. Typical kids are just waiting for you to ease up or forget. Be faithful to the decision to lead your family well.

> The most powerful thing we can do is pray. When you give your burdens to God and ask Him for wisdom, He is faithful to supply it.

Toddlers/Preschoolers

> Children this age are just learning about obedience. If they won't obey, give them a consequence like a time-out. Be consistent and encouraging.

> Take one day a week and do a random act of kindness for someone else. It's fun, and it will also begin to

show your child the joy of giving to others without getting anything in return.

Elementary

> We play our own version of the game Would You Rather? with our kids by asking them questions. Sometimes our kids need to think about how consequences and actions relate. Here are some suggested questions:

> > What if you didn't study for your big test. What would you do?
> > What if you forgot your lunch again. What would you do?
> > What if the ball you threw broke the neighbors' window. What would you do?
> > What if you found the perfect scarf but you didn't have money for it because you forgot to do your chores. What would you do?

Tweens/Teens

> Resist the urge to bail your child out, especially if it's a repeat offense like being forgetful or irresponsible. When it occurs, tell them you love them, but no. Wait for the teachable moment after the fact.
> Expect work from your kids. They are old enough and capable enough to contribute significantly to helping run your household. Let them. It teaches them responsibility, and in return, they might just be a little more grateful for all you do.

CHAPTER 7

LIVING OUT GOD'S LOVE
IN YOUR HOME

ONCE A MONTH, our church family has a meal together. The staff sets up big round tables with only one rule—eat with someone you don't know. I love it because not only do we get to visit with new friends and eat delicious barbecue, it's also a night off from the kitchen. At one of these meals, after Madison had scanned the room, she leaned over and asked me if I'd seen a certain family lately.

"No, I think they are taking the month off. They've had a really difficult time in their family," I replied as I took a big bite of coleslaw.

"What? How do you take a month off from church? People can *do* that?"

I was glad I had swallowed the coleslaw because the shocked look on her face made me laugh.

In twenty years of marriage, Terrell and I have rarely missed a Sunday or Wednesday service at church, and when we do, it's often because we're speaking on behalf of our nonprofit at another church. I wasn't sure if Madison thought our missing church friends were heathens or if she was a little envious.

Her question made me think how much I want my kids to know we faithfully attend church because we want the fellowship, we want to worship with the body of Christ, and we enjoy this part of our week. These are definitely benefits of a Christ-centered home, but checking church off the list, or having a Christian channel as a radio preset, or hanging a cross in our home doesn't make us followers of Jesus.

Checking church off the list, or having a Christian channel as a radio preset, or hanging a cross in our home doesn't make us followers of Jesus.

As a parent, more than anything else, I want my kids to follow Christ. It's higher on my list than success, happiness, financial stability, and education. I don't want them to attend church out of habit or duty. I want them to have a deep, abiding relationship with Him because I'm convinced this is the only road to contentment, true success, and happiness in life. I don't know what the future holds for Madison, Jon-Avery, and Emerson. I can't foresee the joy and pain they will find on life's path. I can't predict the victories and the earth-shattering defeats. I can't always protect them, but Jesus can. He can be with them in life when I can't be. And He will walk with them in every season. At the end of my life, I want Psalm 127:1 to be my legacy: "Unless the LORD builds the house, those who build it labor in vain" (ESV).

Just as God's Word tells us we can't serve two masters, we

also can't be divided in our central focus, finding ourselves caught choosing between our children and God. There can only be one center. It's something pastor and author William Farley stresses in his book *Gospel-Powered Parenting*:

> It is important to love your children, but there is a fine line between healthy parental love and child worship. We know the latter has happened when we begin compromising God's will for the sake of our children or their activities. . . . Compromise always points to idolatry. It displeases God. He does not like competitors, especially when they are our children.[1]

I don't think there's a magic formula or a parenting book that can tell us how to raise Christ-followers. If there were, I would buy it (instead of trying to write it). I believe it's a combination of many things: a strong foundation, consistency, trial and error, and ultimately, a child who chooses to be a Christ-follower.

But I know it doesn't happen by accident; a Christ-centered home starts with us as parents. It involves intentionality and hard work, and this begins with inviting Jesus to be part of our lives.

Asked to define a "Christ-centered home," Focus on the Family responded,

> One thing's certain: it's *not* a home governed by dead, restrictive "religious" rules.

A Christ-centered home starts with us as parents. It involves intentionality and hard work and inviting Jesus to be part of our lives.

Instead, it's a place where family members live their lives under the "bright shadow" of the presence of the Son of God—where people speak and act and relate to one another in the awareness that Jesus Himself is an intimately concerned participant in everything they do. It's a household of which it can truly be said, "Christ is the Head of this house, the Unseen Guest at every meal, the Silent Listener to every conversation."[2]

When Terrell and I were youth pastors, we got a call at nine o'clock one evening from a family in our church. The parents were having a crisis with one of their teens and asked if we would come over. Our two-year-old marriage and Bible school degree didn't prepare us for what we were about to walk into. I'll never forget stepping into that tense situation with a sixteen-year-old rebellious daughter standing on the stairs with bags packed. Her parents had told her she would have to leave if she was going to continue to sleep with her boyfriend. So she packed a bag and was ready to walk out the door.

There was yelling and crying, and they wanted us to fix it. They wanted the youth pastors to reconcile their daughter to them and to Christ. We were asked to do an impossible job. Somehow we managed to get everyone talking—at least while we were there. When we finally left after midnight, we were just glad she had decided to stay at home that night, and we encouraged the family to get into counseling. As we drove home, I realized their story had started long before it climaxed that night. We later learned that the teen's father was in the middle of an extramarital affair, which obviously affected the daughter's disrespectful behavior. Parents say much more to their kids by their lives than by their words.

GOD'S INSTRUCTIONS TO PARENTS

In Deuteronomy 6:6-9, Moses gave God's instructions to the Israelites about parents' responsibility to teach their children absolute truths. These instructions still apply to parents today. And not just on Sundays for an hour at church.

> These words that I am giving you today are to be in your heart. Repeat them to your children. Talk about them when you sit in your house and when you walk along the road, when you lie down and when you get up. Bind them as a sign on your hand and let them be a symbol on your forehead. Write them on the doorposts of your house and on your gates. (HCSB)

I love how Alvin Reid, professor of evangelism at Southeastern Baptist Theological Seminary, divides this passage into six parts,[3] which is helpful when we are trying to create ways to practice each part in our home:

1. *"These words that I am giving you today are to be in your heart."* I want my kids to catch me reading my Bible early in the morning and overhear my off-key worship in the shower. I want them to know that I pray for them every day. I love it when they ask if they can purchase a worship song off iTunes that they've heard at church. I want the gospel to grow

deep into their hearts. After youth camp, my son and his best friend challenged each other to read ten chapters of the Bible a day, starting in Matthew. I loved their ambitious goal, but I was glad they changed it to two chapters a few days later. It seems pretty remarkable to me that two thirteen-year-old boys would text to keep each other accountable on Bible reading. And it's important because God's living Word will not return void.

2. *"Repeat them to your children."* While it's never too late to focus our homes on Jesus, if we can start when our kids are young, we might be able to avoid some of life's hardships that come when we focus on ourselves. Starting when they are young, it's vital that we teach our children right from wrong, obedience, unconditional love, and how to look at the world through God's lens and not the world's. I have also felt compelled to instill integrity in my children by teaching them God's standard of holiness as it relates to sexual purity, marriage, and life, so they can compare everything they are exposed to in the world to Him. Everyone has a worldview, whether they realize it or not. I agree with Alvin Reid that a parent "should help [children] see how to live out a biblical worldview, making decisions in all arenas of life from a biblical perspective. [We] should not raise them to be faithful citizens in a religious subculture, but to see all of creation with biblical eyes."[4]

3. *"Talk about them when you sit in your house."* One of the most important things we've ever done to create

a Christ-centered home was turning our family mealtime into an opportunity to break another kind of bread. Reading Scripture together, talking about it, writing verses in notebooks, and even discussing our differences of opinion have shaped our family. It has become a time to connect and grow. It has made the Word of God an important component of our home. It hasn't always gone smoothly, but we've kept trying because it matters, even when it's messy.

> *Reading Scripture together, talking about it, writing verses in notebooks, and even discussing differences of opinion have shaped our family.*

4. *"When you walk along the road."* Making Christ the central focus of our lives means taking Him wherever we go. We don't pull Him out just for Sundays or for praying over meals. He is our best friend and He is always with us. This is such a valuable truth to teach our kids because we can't be with them for every test or challenge they face. We know that Jesus sticks closer than a brother when we take Him wherever we go. And as Alvin Reid says, we shouldn't keep Him to ourselves. "Simply talking to our neighbors about things that matter helps children see the world through missionary eyes. Talk about Jesus in everyday life."[5]

5. *"When you lie down and when you get up."* Morning and bedtime routines are a great time to begin and end our days with prayer. Children respond to this kind of consistency. Emerson has always loved this

time, and even though for years her prayers were mostly repetition, this is how she learned to pray. Reid points out, "One *Lifeway* study showed that 88% of Christian families never prayed together . . . regularly. We can hardly complain about prayer being taken from the public schools if we are not praying in our Christian homes."[6]

6. *"Bind them as a sign on your hand and let them be a symbol on your forehead. Write them on the doorposts of your house and on your gates."* If you visited our house, you would see that we take this command literally. I love home décor that inspires my family. But I think this Scripture is about more than just the physical act of writing or hanging up some spiritually inspiring item—it's about making the very essence of who we are as a family about Jesus.

So yes. That's basically all the time. I spent my first years of parenting adding Jesus to our home and lives like salt and pepper to season it—a dash here, a sprinkle there. It wasn't necessarily wrong, but it also wasn't enough because our focus was still on us—what we wanted to do, to have, to be. We were cocooned from the world. It wasn't until our marriage went through a troubled

We had been guilty of fitting Jesus into our lives, instead of fitting our lives into Jesus.

season that I realized our focus was out of whack. That trial of hitting rock bottom caused us to look at our foundation, where we discovered some cracks. Instead of fitting Jesus into our lives, we began to fit our lives into Jesus. And we started the shift from a child- (and self-) centered home to a Jesus-centered one.

MARKS OF A CHRIST-CENTERED HOME

Focus on the Family breaks their definition of a Christ-centered home into six parts.

> *Joy* is characteristic of a truly Christian home. . . .
> A Christian home is *orderly*. As the apostle Paul says,
> "God is not the author of confusion but of peace"
> (1 Corinthians 14:33). . . . A Christ-centered home
> should be marked by *grace* [and be] a place of *service*.
> A Christ-centered home is a place where the *spiritual
> disciplines* are practiced. . . . Finally, a Christian
> home is based on *God's purposes* for every member of
> the household.[7]

I couldn't agree more! Let's look more closely at these six areas.

First, we all know our kids can't be happy all the time. But joy is a unique expression of happiness because it comes from God; it is abiding and not dependent on circumstances. So even if we have temporarily unhappy kids, there can be a sense of joy in our home.

I love order in my house. And because we serve a God of order, we can lean on Him to bring peace, even in the hardest times. There have been countless times when I've had parenting struggles with my kids (generally after I've told them no) that I've prayed for peace and order to reign in our home.

Early on in our parenting journey, Terrell and I attended

Pine Cove, a Christian family camp, and Tim Kimmel was the speaker. I hadn't read any of his books and didn't even know who he was. His grace-based parenting lessons changed the way we parented from that week forward. Grace to allow our kids to fail and struggle is a sign of Christ being the center of our homes.

When it comes to service, since we started our nonprofit in 2010, our family has logged thousands of serving hours. There are just so many opportunities. But as many families have discovered, it's not nearly as fun to serve others who live under the same roof. I know we are on the right track when my kids serve from their hearts.

Next, a Christ-centered home requires practicing spiritual disciplines. When it comes to reading Scripture together after our meals and attending church as a family, we rarely make exceptions. We work hard to be consistent and disciplined in this area. There was a short season when one of my kids was having struggles with faith. The teen years are often a time to question and even reject everything parents embrace. We let our teen ask hard questions about our faith—some we couldn't answer (such as "What if God isn't real? Why don't I feel Him more?")—and we listened. But we still required attendance around the table and at church. We had some bumpy days, but we remained faithful to our commitment to make Christ the top priority. That's not to say all our challenges are behind us, but our kids understand what our expectations are.

Finally, a Christian home is founded upon God's purposes. What is His purpose? It's for us to make His glory known in our lives, homes, and ultimately, the world, so that others may see our good works and glorify God in heaven (Matthew 5:16).

If you think Christ-centered homes are perfect or sinless—ha! They are far from it. I think this is where I feel most defeated as a parent. Even though we try to keep Jesus at the center of our home, at those times when all hell breaks loose with tantrums and tempers, Terrell and I feel like complete failures.

We struggle with this regularly, especially during Advent season. Last year, I was determined to make Advent with my family perfect. Just imagine the setting with me: sacred Christmas music in the background, my family sitting down together to enjoy a delicious home-cooked meal, polite conversation with one person asking another how his or her day went, and one of us creating a long list of our blessings. We would listen intently to the daily reading, reflect quietly as we pondered the truth, and then gather around our Jesse Tree[8] to place the first ornament on it together.

The truth was that on the first night of Advent last year, we ended up eating overpriced sandwiches at Schlotzsky's across from our church because our kids were running late for youth group. We threw in a lovely family fight for good measure—complete with teen eye rolls, tween grumbling, and whining from the whole lot. By the time I remembered Ann Voskamp's family Advent book,[9] which I had tucked into my purse at the last minute, I felt like a failure.

Failure is good at convincing us it's too late for anything before we even start.

I'm pretty sure everyone sighed loudly when they saw me pull it out. Failure is good at convincing us it's too late for anything before we even start. Terrell pushed through and read Ann's words in *Unwrapping the Greatest Gift* aloud in that sandwich shop: "There was this family—Jesse's family. A family that was like yours . . . a family that loved each other and hurt each other and forgave each other and failed each other. A family that failed God. . . . They failed and fell and were like a fallen tree."[10]

I smiled at him as he read on about the miraculous shoot springing up from that hopeless family stump. "Out of the stump came one tender branch that would grow right into a crown of thorns, right into a rugged cross, right into a ladder—your ladder back to God."[11] I swallowed my frustration as I heard the first few sentences; I didn't remember my failure, I remembered what God could do with it.

A MOTHER'S WORDS OF WISDOM

A few weeks later on a visit to my in-laws' farm over the holidays, I was confessing to Betty, my mother-in-law, how inadequate I felt as a parent. "I just feel that in some ways, we're on the homestretch with our older kids. At sixteen and thirteen, they are old enough to make good decisions or hide the bad ones."

My mother-in-law didn't dispute or disagree with my words. Instead she encouraged me with a couple of stories about her kids—Terrell and his sisters, Ladonna and Rhonda—who turned out to be not only good people, but more important, Christ-followers. (Our family lost Rhonda unexpectedly in 2013 but we are looking forward to seeing her again.)

When Rhonda was a teenager, she went through a rebellious streak. One night, she went on a date with a boy she knew her parents wouldn't approve of. Halfway through the evening, she knew she'd gotten in over her head with this guy she hardly knew.

At home, Betty was folding laundry late at night when she had a strong urge to stop and pray for Rhonda right then and there. When Rhonda got home, she threw herself into her mom's arms, saying, "Mom, were you praying for me tonight? The date turned bad, and I was asking God for help. I will never do that again!"

And then Betty told me about the time Terrell was a senior in high school and woke her and her husband up at midnight one night to confess that he had been struggling with temptation and had decided to break up with his girlfriend. It was a pivotal night for Terrell, when he was brave enough to let his parents into the secrets of his heart.

Betty looked at me and said, "Pray for your children, Kristen. Give them to God." Her words were comforting and yet kind of scary because in some ways, our job is nearing an end. We've taught and educated, disciplined and discipled our kids. Now our authority has shifted to influence.

TAKING OFF THE TRAINING WHEELS

When our children are small, we can physically control them. We can keep them out of danger with a baby gate and put them in the confines of a crib. As they grow, our physical control lessens and we begin using our authority to teach them obedience by giving consequences and praise. Once kids hit the tween and teen years, our authority should begin to lessen while our influence grows. We watched this principle in action with the person who introduced the concept to us, Mike Dickenson, a pastor Terrell and I worked for before we had children. His boys are grown men now, but watching Mike and his wife parent their teens with influence instead of authority made a profound impact on us.

A year ago, when Jon-Avery was twelve, he went to a classmate's house to work on a school science fair project. There were several boys in the group, all good friends. They finished the project about forty-five minutes earlier than expected and decided to play video games until their parents came to pick them up.

Once kids hit the tween and teen years, our authority should begin to lessen while our influence grows.

Jon-Avery called to tell me exactly that. "Mom, they are going to play *Call of Duty*. Can I play it?"

It was a loaded question because Jon-Avery knew we didn't allow him to own teen-rated games. At the same time, he was with his peers—all great kids I knew. I could sense the pressure he was feeling behind his words. He knew where I stood on the issue, but he also knew from similar situations in the past that we wouldn't condemn him. We wouldn't have even known about the video game if he hadn't told us.

"Son, you are old enough to make this decision. Do what you think is best. I can pick you up if you'd like or you can stay longer," I said, and we hung up.

I could have exerted my authority, but instead I used my influence. In this situation, I don't think there was a clear right or wrong. At his age, I certainly didn't feel like it would damage him to play the game for a few minutes.

When I arrived at the prearranged time and he got in the car next to me, he said, "I decided not to play. I don't really like those kinds of games. It just didn't feel right." He grew up a little more because he made the decision for himself.

I'm just getting into the teen years with my older two, and I'm learning this whole influence over authority thing is hard. I like control. I like being in authority, but I'm learning that when I throw my authority around, it makes my kids want to run further from me and not to me. And let's face it, it's hard to let our kids grow up because we know they are going to make mistakes and learn some lessons the hard way. But it's necessary. As our kids become teenagers, it's critical that we begin to shift how we discipline and interact with them.

I love how Tedd Tripp identifies the three stages of child development in *Shepherding a Child's Heart*:

Ages 0 to 5: focus is establishing biblical authority
Ages 5 to 12: focus is on the development of godly character
Ages 12 and beyond: focus is on internalization of the gospel[12]

I think it's important that our teens understand we don't give them what they deserve when they make mistakes. If any of us received what we really deserved, it would be a rough ending. We offer grace, love, patience, and forgiveness to them because that's what Jesus Christ offers to us. As our children get older, they begin to transition slowly into adulthood and understand this truth even more.

I began to see this shift when my kids got into junior high school. I had less control over every aspect of their lives—from social interactions to turning in homework. I was still an authority and could make them obey, but I often discovered that if I left the choice up to them, they owned the results, even if it meant failure or disappointment.

Blogger Jay Younts in his comments on Tripp's book says, "Stressing authority in the teenage years obscures the message of the gospel and puts the focus of the teenager on the behavior of his parents. Authority in this context equates to correcting and controlling behavior."[13]

LEARNING TO CONNECT

I've bitten my tongue time and again with Madison, my oldest child. Sometimes I feel bad for her because I'm still learning how to parent and she's my test case. We are both headstrong and can clash with our passionate opinions. I spend a lot of time apologizing. But when I can hush up and let her choose her path, I'm usually happy with the direction she chooses. Oh yes, and I pray for wisdom—a lot.

One night after a particularly rough day when we couldn't seem to see eye to eye on anything, I saw this played out. I was making the rookie mistake of exercising authority instead of influence. I really wanted her to step out of her comfort zone with some girls her age, and I was pushing her to do something I wanted and I thought she needed. I curled up in her bed and when I just let her talk, I got to the heart of her issue: She was feeling insecure and was struggling with self-esteem issues. When I really listened and left the decision up to her, I discovered she didn't need me to fix her problems. I couldn't anyway. I did the only thing I knew might help: I pointed her to Jesus. I prayed with her. I cried with her. I said, "Madison, Jesus cares about this. Lay this burden at His feet."

When I returned to her room later to drop off something, I found her listening to worship music and wiping away tears from talking to God. I realized in that moment that this is the essence of a Christ-centered home—not getting it right the first or even the tenth time, but inviting Jesus in and letting Him heal our hearts and guide our lives.

The following week, Madison spent some time with those same girls and had a great time. I think it was partly because she made the decision on her own.

While I don't think there is a hard-and-fast formula for great parenting, someone once told me:

1. Correct kids when they are young (birth to elementary).
2. Direct them as they grow (middle school, junior high).
3. Connect with them as they get older (high school and on).

I've always tried to remember those simple suggestions.

My agent, Bill Jensen, and I spent hours talking about this book and our roles as parents. One day over coffee, I pulled out my phone and typed these words he said: "Our job as parents is to raise our kids to be responsible adults so they can discern good from evil, beauty from ugliness, and truth from error." If we can accomplish this, we've done our jobs.

So what are some ways to create a Jesus-centered home?

In *Gospel-Powered Parenting*, author William Farley mentions the attributes of a life of "God-centeredness," and I think we can easily apply these to our homes. He says the first thing is telling our kids no when it is in their best interest. Second, Dad and Mom should be united in front of their kids. Third, we need to allow marriage to come before the children. And as he says, "God-centered homes will be radically different."[14]

When I was working on this chapter, Jon-Avery asked me what I was writing about. When I told him, he said, "Are you going to tell them that our Christ-centered home sometimes has yelling and fighting?" I assured him that I already had. I thought about his words and how important they were because I think sometimes we feel like if we're centering everything around Jesus, we will live in perfect harmony. Our family is living proof of the opposite. Even when Jesus' disciples were walking with Him on earth, there wasn't always harmony. It's so critical that we understand that parenting is hard, especially when we are trying to keep Jesus at the center of it.

I think the bottom line is that Christ-centered homes won't all look the same. We all have different convictions and passions and will establish our homes accordingly. But Christ-centered homes keep Him at the center. Everything flows from that focus, and that gives us a strong common thread with other believers.

GOING AGAINST THE FLOW

Parents
It goes without saying that we have a heavy responsibility to lead our children. While that may seem an

obvious generalization, we can take simple, practical steps to do so:

> Prepare ourselves spiritually. It's hard to be a spiritual leader if we are running on empty.
> Read the Bible together as a family.
> Pray together over small worries, not just big needs.
> Have regular family nights.
> Live what you teach your kids.
> Model love and forgiveness with your spouse.
> Create a safe atmosphere in which kids can learn, grow, and mess up.

Toddlers/Preschoolers

> Make a prayer collage with pictures of friends and family who need prayer.
> Establish a devotion time early on by reading together from an age-appropriate Bible or a Bible storybook.

Elementary

> Occasionally ask your kids to lead a family devotion or read to the family from *The Jesus Storybook Bible*[15] or another resource.
> Discuss character traits of people in the Bible whom we can look to or learn from.
> Look for teachable moments and use them to direct your kids back to the Cross.
> Each month, memorize a verse together.

Tweens/Teens

> Ask your teens to share the top five priorities in their lives. Get them talking and then listen. Don't correct or overreact if God or faith doesn't make their list. Share your list with them.

> Write a note to your teen and leave it in his or her room, giving praise for a recent good decision. It's so easy to focus on the bad ones, but thanking our kids for showing character in a tough situation will encourage more of those choices.

PART IV

WHITE WATER

Talk about countercultural. In a world where everything
revolves around yourself—protect yourself, promote yourself, comfort
yourself, and take care of yourself—Jesus says, "Crucify yourself.
Put aside all self-preservation in order to live for God's glorification,
no matter what that means for you in the culture around you."

DAVID PLATT

CHAPTER 8

GRATITUDE IS A CHOICE

LAST CHRISTMAS, we surprised Jon-Avery with a fair trade djembe drum from Africa. Not only did our budding percussionist enjoy making beautiful rhythmic music with his hands, our purchase empowered an artisan from the Ivory Coast.

I lost count of how many times Jon-Avery sought out Terrell and me to say thank you. A djembe wasn't something he'd asked for, but he appreciated the gift so much and wanted us to know he was grateful.

Each of our kids said thank you for their Christmas presents as they opened them, but I could tell Jon-Avery felt deep gratitude because he tried for days to convey how much the gift meant. At one point, he said, "Mom, I don't deserve this. I feel so rich."

"You are," I responded. "Not because you have a new drum to beat on, but because you're grateful."

His words made me think of Ben Stein's reflection on his father's thankfulness to have had a job as a college student washing dishes in a fraternity house. "I cannot tell you anything that, in a few minutes, will tell you how to be rich. But I can tell you how to feel rich, which is far better. . . . Be grateful. . . . As my pal Phil DeMuth says, it's the only totally reliable get-rich-quick scheme."[1]

I think Jon-Avery's initial thank-you turned to deep gratitude because of grace. For whatever reason, he saw the gift as undeserved merit.

The scientific and medical benefits of gratitude are renowned. There have been more than twenty-six studies on the science of gratitude, and there is medical proof that it makes us healthier.[2] Robert Emmons, codirector of the Gratitude project at the Greater Good Science Center (GGSC), University of California Berkeley, adds his voice to the discussion. In his book *Thanks! How the New Science of Gratitude Can Make You Happier*, Emmons says, "When I am grateful, I recognize that I have no claim on the gift or benefit I received; it was freely bestowed out of compassion, generosity, or love."[3] He observes that grace and gratitude flow into one another. "Perceive grace and you will naturally feel gratitude. Grace is unearned. It's a free gift."[4]

Thank you.

Nothing makes a parent's heart explode with joy like these unprompted words from our kids. We revel in them; we replay them in our minds. We take our kids' gratitude to heart. It makes us feel like we are doing something right.

And nothing makes us more discouraged than when the words never come. When the opportunity to say thank you dies before it's seized, it makes us feel like failures. I've waited, given the look, cleared my throat, and asked for thanksgiving. But we all know forced gratitude isn't quite the same.

"Thank you." Nothing makes a parent's heart explode with joy like these unprompted words from our kids. Or makes us more discouraged when the words never come.

Perhaps that's why the unprompted thank-yous mean so much. Maybe that's why my son's heartfelt desire to express gratitude is something I remember every time I hear him beat his drum.

I have good kids—actually, great kids. They probably aren't any less grateful than most. But they still need reminding and prodding. They need discipline and redirection.

At our house, dinnertime plus the twenty minutes after we eat is a time for our family to connect. I've long said it's the most important time of our day. It can also be the most stressful—togetherness will do that to you. Most nights we take turns talking about our highs and lows of the day—the good and the bad. We usually read some Scripture together, work on a Discovery Bible Study (where we write down Scripture and talk about its meaning), or read from a devotional book.

One month last year, we decided to memorize Psalm 23 (I'll tell you why in a minute). We started with the first verse and repeated it over and over. "The LORD is my shepherd, I shall not want." I asked the kids, "Do you know what this means?" Jon-Avery talked about sheep and a shepherd's job.

Emerson added that sheep were dumb. I explained that "I shall not want" means we have everything we need and we should be content with what we have. Madison was getting irritated with the slow and babyish way we were memorizing, but nobody calls Emerson a baby without a fight. Long story short, in less than five minutes two out of three of my children were either crying or screaming on the way to their rooms.

"Well, that went well," I told Terrell.

I felt so defeated trying to teach my kids about contentment with so much discontentment in the room.

It turns out the better lesson was about to be learned. Emerson returned after some time in her room and offered an unprompted heartfelt apology—the kind that gets your attention because you know it's the real deal. Madison and I texted for a while, and she did the same.

She also asked me about the bag of clothes a friend of mine had dropped off. They were very nice hand-me-downs she passed down to Madison from her daughter. I was tempted to not give them to her (petty, yes, but I was still looking for the lesson here). "I want you to be content with what you have, honey," I said, as I handed her the sack.

An hour later, she brought it down to me—full. "I filled it with my own clothes for us to pass on to someone else. I am grateful, Mom."

I thought of the words to the Twenty-third Psalm and knew they'd found their mark without my "help."

When entitlement's poison begins to infect our hearts, gratitude is the antidote.

"In all its manifestations, a preoccupation with the self can cause us to forget our benefits and our benefactors or to feel that we are owed things from others and therefore have no reason to feel thankful," claims Emmons. "Counting blessings will be ineffective because grievances will always outnumber gifts."[5]

When entitlement's poison begins to infect our hearts, gratitude is the antidote.

Emmons wants us to realize that we did not create ourselves—we were created. Likewise, we are never truly self-sufficient. We need some people to grow our food and others to heal our injuries; we need love, and we look to God, family, partners, friends, and pets to fill that.

"Seeing with grateful eyes requires that we see the web of interconnection in which we alternate between being givers and receivers," writes Emmons. "The humble person says that life is a gift to be grateful for, not a right to be claimed."[6]

We aren't born feeling grateful; rather, when we are born, we quickly begin to feel entitled to our parents' care. Gratitude is learned. Christine Carter, a sociologist and happiness expert at UC Berkeley's Greater Good Parents program, says that gratitude and happiness are so closely associated they are hard to distinguish from each other. She suggests that simply counting our blessings in a routine way works wonders.[7]

I think the key to raising grateful kids is maintaining gratitude. (I need help too. How often have I given thanks to God or someone else and then turned around and complained or asked for more with the next breath?) Creating a routine filled with consistent opportunity for gratitude helps us maintain it. And it can be as simple as writing down what we are thankful for each day.

Maintaining gratitude is challenging because our situations, circumstances, and emotions change like the weather. But God is always the same. He never changes. Numbers 23:19 reminds us of this truth: "God is not human, that he should lie, not a human being, that he should change his mind. Does he speak and then not act? Does he promise and not fulfill?" And Hebrews 13:8 assures us why we can put our trust in Jesus: "Jesus Christ is the same yesterday and today and forever." If nothing else, that unshakable promise—that God never wavers in His promises to us even when we stumble along in our obedience to Him—is something to be thankful for each and every day.

Creating a routine filled with consistent opportunity for gratitude—such as writing down what we are thankful for each day—helps us maintain it.

PERSPECTIVE CHANGES EVERYTHING

"We need to find a place to serve."

I whispered these words to my husband five days after Christmas.

He nodded his head. He could hear the kids arguing and nit-picking upstairs too. Ah, Christmas break. Presents had been worn, plugged in, and played with, and a dose of perspective was next on the list.

Twenty-four hours later, we sat on a blue tarp in inner-city Houston with a bunch of kids at a Sidewalk Sunday School after-school event.

It was so cold it didn't take long for children we didn't know to crawl into our laps and lean close for warmth. Terrell passed out the extra sweatshirts and throw blanket we keep in the car. My kids scattered in the crowd and found new friends to keep warm with.

Pastor Scott, the faithful man who drives his colorful truck to low-income apartment complexes nearly every day of the week to teach children about Jesus, told the children to sit still, listen closely, and cup their opened hands in their laps for the blessing they were about to receive. I looked over at Emerson sitting in between girls she had just met. I got a lump in my throat when I saw her little hands cupped, waiting for her blessing.

I'm pretty sure she was hoping to catch the small toys and candy that Pastor Scott always brings, just like the rest of the kids. And I couldn't blame her really.

But then she leaned over and whispered, "If I catch anything, I'm going to give it away to the other kids," and I wanted to shout, *"Yes!"* Looking around at her peers without shoes and coats, she could see her hands were already full.

Nothing makes us more grateful than perspective.

I wasn't reminding and prodding and nagging her to be grateful—she knew she already had everything she needed. Nothing makes us more grateful than perspective. *Nothing.* I think it's the key to loosening the chains of entitlement in our culture.

It's not just kids who need a regular dose of perspective. I'll never forget going to a party at a friend's house and walking through the massive entryway, mouth agape at the extravagantly beautiful home with fine furnishings and even finer art. My first thought was, *This is spectacular,* and my second thought was, *This is way better than what I have.*

On the way home, I said as much to Terrell. His response left me speechless. "I bet if our friends in Kenya came to a party at our house, they would say the same thing."

Yes. It all depends on whom we compare ourselves to.

The lesson was brought home even more clearly one night as I got Emerson ready for bed and she grumbled about a new toy she wanted. "Everyone has one, Mom," she whined.

"Well, do you think Ephantus [one of the children we've sponsored for years through Compassion International] has one?"

She thought quietly. "No, his house isn't even as big as my room." I knew she was remembering our visit to his Kenyan home the summer before.

"Yes, that's right," I said gently, and as I said the following words aloud, I said them for my benefit as much as hers. "Honey, it's okay to want things we don't have, but we also need to remember all we do have. If we are going to compare ourselves to those who have more, we must also compare ourselves to those who have less."

Since maintaining gratitude is so challenging, I'm constantly looking for ways to change my family's perspective. It's just too easy to become ungrateful in our culture, where wants and needs have been confused. It's natural to compare ourselves to those around us—and if you live in North America like I do, you and your kids are comparing yourselves to some of the wealthiest people in the world. Perspective helps us compare ourselves to the world, whose inhabitants often live much differently than we do.

KEYS TO MAINTAINING GRATITUDE

One of the best ways to change perspective is to seize every opportunity to serve others. Last summer, my teens spent a week in the hot Texas sun as counselors at our church's kids' camp. They had a blast singing crazy camp songs, cheering, and high-fiving the young campers under their charge. They tied shoes, passed out Band-Aids, and encouraged campers with homesick hearts. For an entire week, they put others' needs before their own.

Madison and Jon-Avery came home with barely their voices and a load of stinky laundry and fell into bed for a five-hour nap.

At the dinner table that night, reenergized, the two begged us to let them go on the youth group missions trip a few weeks later to help with construction projects for some marginalized people in a Texas community. We didn't really have it budgeted or planned so I said no. The disappointment was evident on their faces.

Later, Terrell pulled me aside and said, "Honey, let's rethink this. Our kids just came back from a week serving others, and instead of complaining about all the work, they are asking for more. I know it will cost us some extra money, but the outcome for our kids could be priceless."

He was right. When we told our kids we were reconsidering, they offered to contribute some of their own money. I knew something good was going to come from this.

They left on a Sunday, and the first update from my daughter read, "Mom! We just finished our first day of hard work. Today was so hot and we are so tired. We are giving this lady a new floor so we had to rip out the old one, leaving a huge hole, and then add new supports, more flooring, and then tiles. It was a lot of work but it was fun! Love you."

I got only one text from my son all week. "Mom, I love you. The week has been amazing! We just washed each other's feet and now we're at Dairy Queen. Serving rocks!"

Yes, my kids worked their tails off as temporary construction workers, enjoying every minute of it. They were being changed from the inside out and probably didn't even realize it. Here's what my kids learned:

1. You don't think about yourself when you're busy thinking about others.
2. You are thankful for things you take for granted. Hello, a floor.
3. You feel good about yourself. Can you hear the pride in my daughter's text?
4. You want to keep doing it. Serving is contagious.
5. You can have fun in the midst of hard work.
6. You understand that whatever you do for others matters.

Another way we maintain gratitude is with consistency. We learn by habit and through repetition, and the best way to live grateful lives is to practice gratitude. We also try to incorporate perspective in our daily routine, such as dinner. For more than a year, we've (mostly) eaten the exact same thing one day a week.

Sometimes the best way to introduce a different perspective is by doing something different.

We aren't in a culinary rut. It's not something gourmet, and there aren't any secret ingredients. But it's intentional.

We eat rice and beans every Monday so we can remember how the rest of the world lives and eats. Sometimes the best way to introduce a different perspective is by doing something different. And then repeating it often.

Most of the world doesn't have the luxury of having a pantry and refrigerator full of food with dozens of options. Meat is for the wealthy and fruit is a delicacy.

What better way to remind our kids how much we have than through their bellies?

A few months into this routine, when one of the kids asked, "What's for dinner?" my response—"It's Monday"— was met with a groan.

"Mom, I'm sick of rice and beans. Can we please stop?" My family *likes* rice and beans. (Our favorite recipe follows— a pretty no-fuss meal, wouldn't you agree?) But I was waiting for the moment they stopped liking them because that's when the real lesson is learned.

Recipe

Cook brown rice, lightly salt, add freshly chopped cilantro.

Top with a generous amount of black beans, seasoned with cumin.

Add fresh avocado.

No, we haven't stopped eating rice and beans yet—because it matters. For us, it is a constant reminder that we are blessed to have something on our plates.

We all need gratitude training. Here are some ideas that can help:

1. *Write down what you're thankful for as a family.* Robert Emmons encourages gratitude-seekers to keep a gratitude journal.[8] I'm mentioning this simple idea again because it's too important to ignore. Something powerful happens when we write down what we are thankful for. Keep a family or personal gratitude journal—decorate the family version together. Create a gratitude memo or bulletin board to display photos, objects, and so forth, or write out your thanks on notepaper to read aloud and pin on the board later. Whatever your method, do it. You won't be sorry.

2. *Watch your mouth.* Emmons warns that negative talk can influence how we think.[9] We all know the power of words. The Bible says in Proverbs 18:21, "The tongue can bring death or life" (NLT). One week, I noticed our family was really struggling with complaining and speaking negatively. I handed everyone at the table a rubber band and told them to put it around their wrists like a bracelet. We slipped them on as we finished dinner, and I said these words: "Every time you grumble or complain, snap your rubber band." The day before we had memorized John 6:43 at our dinnertime devotions. "Stop grumbling among yourselves." Guess who got the first "pop"? Ouch.

My kids laughed as the first complaint rolled off my tongue just minutes after reading our assignment. I wasn't even trying to show them an example of what not to do. I didn't even know I was going to grumble about cleaning up our dinner mess. Because sometimes complaining is so second nature it slips out before we can catch it.

I rubbed my wrist and watched my words.

Sometimes complaining is so second nature it slips out before we can catch it.

We all did. Our twenty-four-hour experiment proved to leave our wrists a little tender and our tongues a little more controlled. We were listening for the bemoaning and belly-aching. We pointed out when we heard each other complain. The most important thing this experiment did? It made us think before speaking. It made us more aware.

Grumbling comes too easy. And when we try not to do it, we see how often we whine or complain—about each other, about our situations, about what we have and what we don't. When we really get a good look at what's underneath all those negative words, we find ingratitude.

Try this simple lesson today. (If rubber bands won't work for you, keep tally marks on the kitchen calendar. Or put Cheerios around a yarn bracelet and break one off with every complaint.)

Here's what a lesson in complaining less does for all of us:

> It forces us to admit how often we grumble or whine or speak negatively about ourselves or others.
> It causes us to think before we speak.
> It gives us the opportunity to choose gratitude over grumbling.

While this lesson won't necessarily rid our homes of complaining (ask me how I know), it will certainly give us something to think and talk about.

3. *Walk in someone else's shoes.* I'm an introvert who isn't much of a people-person. I like quiet. I like being alone.

That's why it cracks my husband up that over the past five years since starting our nonprofit (which depends heavily on volunteer support), our back door has become a revolving one. One day, Terrell asked me if it bothered me to always have people over. "You used to hate having company," he reminded me. I cringed because it was true.

"I love this change in me. We need so much help. We couldn't do this work without people coming to serve."

I talk a lot in my first book, *Rhinestone Jesus,* and my blog about saying yes to God. Our obedience isn't just for Him; it's for us. He uses it to change us. Since I started writing this book, the family dealing with cancer treatments I mentioned earlier (in chapter 4) has stayed with us half a dozen times. What was first an awkward stretch for this introvert has since become an anticipated visit with dear family friends. Opening up our home to Heather, who has a life-threatening diagnosis, has changed our family. My kids argue over who's giving up his or her room to this precious family—a far cry from where we started. We've collectively held our breaths, waiting to see if Heather's still in remission, because when you walk in someone else's shoes, you can't help but be reminded of your own family's health and all that you have. When my children see Heather missing her kids, they understand she wouldn't choose to be in our home and not hers—and all these things stir up gratitude.

4. *Fill your home with visual reminders and stop to appreciate them.* I love words. My home attests to that fact. It might sound too simple, but putting positive words of Scripture and other affirmations on our walls is a good visual reminder of our goal. Robert Emmons agrees that visual reminders help us not to forget gratitude. We tape them to our mirrors or on the

refrigerator and tuck them in our Bibles as constant reminders. When we moved from a previous home, one of my favorite things to do was read the comments by the other realtors and potential buyers online. Most of the constructive feedback we took to heart, such as moving some extra furniture into the garage to showcase the size of the rooms. I'll never forget one couple's comment, though. It said something to the effect of "This house is different. You can tell this family loves God and serves other people. You can feel it in their home." Since then, I've always hoped to maintain that atmosphere in my house— that even when it's empty, you can tell we are a family that loves God. Terrell reminded me that we wrote in permanent marker in inconspicuous places, like under cabinet and closet shelves, our favorite memories and Scriptures for the new owners to find someday.

We've all heard the saying, "stop and smell the roses," and I think we *should* actually stop and smell the roses. According to Jeremy Smith, "Loyola University psychologist Fred Bryant finds that savoring positive experiences makes them stickier in your brain, and increases their benefits to your psyche—and the key, he argues, is expressing gratitude for the experience. That's one of the ways appreciation and gratitude go hand in hand."[10] When we really slow down and savor the good experiences, the people who have blessed us, and the gifts in our lives, we are choosing gratitude.

5. *Be specific.* One of the habits of highly grateful people, according to Smith, is that they are thankful for the details, or as he puts it, "They mention the pancakes."[11] Grateful people don't just say, "I love you." They say, "I love you because . . ." and they offer instances, the little things that go unnoticed.

When we are specific in our thankfulness, we are more authentic. We take the time to appreciate what we've been given, and it makes a difference. It makes the people in our lives want to continue giving to us because we notice what they do.

6. *Choose gratitude even in your pain.* Oh, this is a hard one. We all know it's easier to be grateful for something good we've been given, but we also know life isn't all good. There are diagnoses and financial struggles and lean years. There are divorces and deaths, and there is despair. Choosing to be thankful in these hard places—this is what sets us free. We are instructed in 1 Thessalonians 5:18 to "give thanks in all circumstances; for this is God's will for you in Christ Jesus." Thankful. All circumstances. God's will. Those are heavy, hard truths. I like what Emmons says in his article "How Gratitude Can Help You through Hard Times": "It's easy to feel grateful for the good things. No one 'feels' grateful that he or she has lost a job or a home or good health or has taken a devastating hit on his or her retirement portfolio."[12]

> *Choosing to be thankful in hard places—this is what sets us free.*

In such moments, he says, gratitude becomes a critical cognitive process—a way of thinking about the world that can help us turn disaster into a stepping-stone. "If we're willing and able to look, . . . we can find a reason to feel grateful even to people who have harmed us. We can thank that boyfriend for being brave enough to end a relationship that wasn't working; the homeless person for reminding us of our advantages and vulnerability; the boss, for forcing us to face new challenges."[13]

I am reminded of another favorite Disney movie, *Meet the Robinsons*, a story of a boy genius who spends a day in the future and discovers an incredible family secret. It's really a movie that celebrates failure because that's how we learn. In fact, one of the characters says, "I propose a toast to Lewis and his brilliant failure. May it lead to success in the future."

There isn't a guidebook for raising grateful kids. We learn because we try. Sure, we fail and get things wrong, but if we keep trying, we also get it right sometimes.

GOING AGAINST THE FLOW

Parents
> Without a doubt, the best way to teach gratitude is to model it.
> Do your kids see you leaving a gratuity at restaurants and writing thank-you notes? How can we expect them to be grateful if we aren't?

Toddlers/Preschoolers
> Research shows that children under the age of seven don't usually spontaneously show gratitude, but they learn it from repetition of observation and prompting.
> Be consistent. Make them ask for things politely and expect a thankful response.

Elementary
> Memorize Psalm 23 as a family. It's only six verses long and can be easily broken into segments to memorize over a month. (I love how it reads in the New Living Translation.)

The LORD is my shepherd;
    I have all that I need.
He lets me rest in green meadows;
    he leads me beside peaceful streams.
    He renews my strength.
He guides me along right paths,
    bringing honor to his name.
Even when I walk
    through the darkest valley,
I will not be afraid,
    for you are close beside me.
Your rod and your staff
    protect and comfort me.
You prepare a feast for me
    in the presence of my enemies.
You honor me by anointing my head with oil.
    My cup overflows with blessings.
Surely your goodness and unfailing love will
      pursue me
    all the days of my life,
and I will live in the house of the LORD
    forever.

> Think of how your Monday night dinners can offer your family a dose of perspective.

Tweens/Teens
> As a mom of two teens (thirteen and sixteen), I need all the help I can get in this area of gratitude. I have learned a few things, one of which is that I need to be

the example. I've learned showing my teens gratitude
for their contributions, no matter how small, goes
a long way. I've also learned to let them express
gratitude in their own way. Madison is grateful,
but sometimes she is slow to show it. If I give her
time and space, she always follows through. My son
is quick to say thank you, but it's more of a reflex.
Neither expression is wrong; what's important is to
accept any and all kinds of gratitude from our kids.
I have also found these points from Christine Carter's
blog *Raising Happiness* to be a great help[14]:

1. Go at it indirectly.
2. Let teens lead.
3. Allow snarkiness, teasing, and humor in expressions
   of gratitude.
4. Use gratitude to cultivate the growth mind-set in
   difficult times.
5. Be persistent.

Gratitude is a choice. Let's choose it today.

CHAPTER 9

WHERE THE RUBBER MEETS THE ROAD

FOR THE FIRST FIVE YEARS of our nonprofit, my husband and I worked out of our office located in a building in our backyard. (The commute was awesome.) There was always someone in that small building packing boxes for Fair Trade Friday, filling orders for the online Mercy House store, and pricing product. Brittany, a mom who helped us part-time by doing a little bit of everything, came every Thursday and Friday. We would leave the back door to the house open so she could use the restroom, grab a drink, or ask a question.

One day as she walked through the house, I was standing at the kitchen counter answering e-mail on my laptop. I started to say something, but I stopped because neither of us could hear the other over Madison practicing her flute in another room. She was working especially hard on some high notes, and I think I inadvertently shuddered. I smiled an apology at Brittany.

Brittany opened the back door in the kitchen to go back to the building, and Jon-Avery was on the back porch shooting archery. Brittany has two toddlers, and we talk a lot about parenting. "Can I ask you a question?" she said when Madison paused. "Are your kids on a schedule? Do you make them practice at a certain time? Every week when I come in the afternoon, Madison is playing her flute and Jon-Avery is busy with archery."

I laughed. "No, they are just both passionate about those things. They practice because they love it and want to improve."

Brittany went back to work, and I stood there in the kitchen thinking about her question and my answer. Like most parents, I've threatened and nagged and forced my kids to practice reading and tying shoes and piano. But I don't have to remind them to practice what they love.

It's true for everyone. For example, I have friends who love cooking. They can't wait to try out new recipes, and they love kitchen gadgets. (For the record, I'm not one of those people.) We enjoy what we enjoy. But life isn't just about what we love; most of the lessons we learn come because of hard work and practice. And sometimes practicing more makes us love something more.

I've researched and written and poured my heart into this book, but without practical application, it's hard to know where to start. How do we shift our homes from entitled to thankful and start the slow process of turning things around? We start with consistency.

For a couple of years now, every Tuesday at four thirty I've taken Emerson to a tumbling class. After discovering her doing flips on the trampoline and constantly "trying new moves," I decided this class was more for her safety than a hobby. But it turns out, she isn't just high-energy and in need of a release valve, she genuinely loves to tumble.

One night at dinner after a lesson, her big sister asked, "What did you do in tumbling today?" Emerson sighed. "The same thing we do every single week." She sounded frustrated, but that's because she can't see what I can.

Yes, she does the same thing over and over, and it feels like she's not getting anywhere, but I can see the consistent practice is making her stronger, sturdier, better. Her coach makes small adjustments and adds minor changes, and she is making progress.

One of the joys of parenting is seeing the progress. I remember when Madison was ten years old and we had just gotten her a flute. Those first few weeks were brutal for everyone as she tried to find the notes on her instrument. Over the years I've driven her to countless lessons, sat in the car waiting for hours, taken freelance jobs to pay for flutes and camps, and bought eight different moisturizers for her dry chin resulting from practicing so much. Only other parents of musicians can understand why I cried when she was named all-area in high school as a freshman flute player. Our family celebrated it with a fancy dinner out at Macaroni Grill.

Let's face it: Parenting is all about practice too. We can't always see the growth—how far we've come—but if we are consistent and if we implement the principles we've learned, we will see change. We get what we put into it.

I have a long list of parenting regrets—snapshots and memories of times when I failed as a mother, and mostly, failed my kids. One is particularly painful. It was the end of the year in middle school, and one of my children had earned a field trip for good grades and behavior. My kids are good, conscientious students so while this wasn't a surprise, it was a treat to miss school and attend this fun event.

We were driving to school, and we were arguing. I don't remember what the fight was about, but I do remember the tone my child had taken, complete with eye rolls and heavy sighs. And it made me furious! Terrell and I had been seeing more and more of this new "attitude," and I wanted to stop it. I told my offending child that one more instance of back talk would earn immediate cancellation of the field trip. Middle school can be frightening for parents because kids are vying for independence, asserting their opinions more, and testing the waters. Hindsight would have shown me that my child's behavior was normal and I needed to respond to the attitude I was detecting (and get to the root of it) instead of react to it.

So, yeah. There were a hundred consequences I could have suggested, but I threatened to take away something that would make the biggest impact. The disrespectful tone appeared again, and I pulled the field trip from under my child's feet as soon as the attitude surfaced. Triumph.

My child begged and pleaded for three days. I wouldn't budge. I was going to be consistent! Privately, I wavered and doubted my decision, and mostly, I regretted suggesting the consequence that would hurt the most.

I wounded my child. So much so that more than a year later, it came up in a family counseling session as one of the biggest hurts in this child's life. I failed as a parent. It was a negative turning point in our personal relationship, and I regretted it.

But I learned it's never too late to apologize. And that's what I did. I confessed my wrongdoing to my child and asked for forgiveness. I would give anything to go back and change what transpired if I could. But I learned something valuable from it: "Winning" a fight with our kids only makes two losers. We have the opportunity to patiently walk with them through their pain and try to understand the root of their attitude or negative behavior. But we have to take it.

Disclaimer: I want practical suggestions for parenting. I go to Google looking for them. I think if you're

Parenting is all about practice. We get what we put into it.

reading this book, you might too. But I'm not a parenting expert—just ask the young people I parent. So please, take my suggestions and what works for us and discover what works for you. My kids aren't perfect and they aren't always grateful. We are learning as we go. No two families are the same. Different things work for different people.

Terrell and I are big advocates of counseling. We benefitted from it when our marriage hit a crisis a decade ago, and we knew it was a good option again when he transitioned from salesman to CEO of Mercy House. As we have been able to budget it, occasional sessions have played a big role in our parenting, too. Money is an issue and not everyone is in a position to afford that kind of professional help. But we prioritize it—not because we are in crisis, but because we love each other and want to invest time and energy to stay in a good place. One of the most impactful tools we've learned (when someone is upset or there's an argument) is to ask the person we are disagreeing with, "What do you need from me right now?" Sometimes it's the best way to get to the root of the problem. I have discovered over and over, my kids and my husband need something different from what I'm offering. Often they're not asking for my opinion or for me to fix their problem; they want me to listen or they just need a hug.

SEVEN STEPS TO RAISING GRATEFUL KIDS
Here are seven areas where we can be consistent and work in practical ways to raise grateful kids instead of entitled ones:

1. We teach ownership.

On our way home from Kenya a couple of summers ago after serving at Mercy House, we had a layover in Amsterdam. We had a short amount of time to see the city with three jet-lagged children. But it was an adventure we all wanted to experience. As our strong-willed firstborn, Madison blossoms in leadership roles. She's determined, thrives on challenges, and doesn't take no for an answer. It's a character strength that I've learned to appreciate. Before we left the States, Terrell dropped a book on her bed that he'd picked up for a dollar at a local thrift store: a guidebook to Amsterdam.

"You're in charge of our two days in Amsterdam. There are maps in the book. Make a list of what we should see." I looked at him like he was crazy.

"Trust me," he whispered. Since I had a lot on my plate getting ready for our trip to Kenya, I did.

Madison, at fourteen, hit the ground running. She navigated us through the transportation web, figured out the most cost-effective way to see the city, picked restaurants I've since dreamed about, and was a most excellent guide. She was in her element because we let her take ownership. And not only did she surprise us, we had a wonderful, memorable trip.

The Amsterdam adventure wasn't the first time we started letting our kids take ownership. Our children became a part of our family economy early on with chores. There are so many ways to involve kids from a very early age in running the household, from toddlers wiping the table to putting the spoons back in the drawer from the dishwasher.

I'll be honest: I come from a long line of control freaks, and often I'd rather do the jobs at home myself because I like them done a certain way lest I end up redoing them. But I believe when I operate in this mode, I rob my family. I take away the opportunity to teach them. We haven't always done things well in this area, and we've lacked consistency, but we continue to try to share the workload at home.

My kids each have four weekly household chores, and each of them helps prepare and clean up after dinner once a week. This is in addition to keeping their rooms clean and taking care of their own laundry. (We started teaching our kids to do their laundry when they were eight years old.) We try to be flexible with schedules and extracurricular events, but for the most part, we are consistent with this. In return for their work, we give them a salary.

Sometimes the lines of ownership get a little blurred in our house, which can be comical. When Madison was in junior high, she was scheduled to have oral surgery to remove several wisdom and permanent teeth, due to impacted baby teeth. She wanted Terrell to document the event on video in case she said anything really honest or funny. On the day of the surgery, after she had received the pre-op anesthetic shots, she did both. At one point in the video, she has drool trickling from the corner of her numbed mouth, with blood-stains on her shirt. As Terrell dabs her mouth, he says, "Oh, honey, you're dripping blood all over your clothes."

Madison looks down and smiles drunkenly. "It's okay. This is Mom's shirt."

Oops. Borrowed somehow turned into ownership in this case. But thankfully it all came out in the wash.

Ultimately, I believe teaching our kids ownership and giving them opportunities to own things creates more responsible, grateful kids. And, in most cases, that requires money.

2. We stress the value of money.

Until our kids started earning money regularly, they generally got it twice a year: birthdays and Christmas from extended family and friends.

The rest of the time, if they wanted anything, they would ask us for money. Go figure.

On this journey of trying to raise grateful kids in an entitled world, we want our children to understand the difference between needs and wants, know how to save a buck, live frugally, and have the means to be generous when the opportunity presents itself. It's tough in a culture that thrives on instant gratification, overspending, and debt.

In my part of the country, many newlyweds skip the apartment rental stage of life and buy a house together, filling its rooms with furniture and accessories from a Pottery Barn catalog. It's not unusual for little girls to have biweekly pedicures. And don't even get me started on hair highlights, fake nails, and hundred-dollar jeans for teens. I'm not saying these things are wrong in themselves, but I do think we're entering dangerous territory when we buy what we can't afford or too much of what we can afford. This easy-finance mentality is passed along to our children.

Even without allowances or iPhones or the "you can have whatever you want" parenting philosophy, we noticed our children were constantly asking for more stuff. I began to realize they didn't understand the importance of a budget, the value of a dollar, or the crucial art of saving because we had never taught them.

After listening to a Focus on the Family podcast with guest speaker Mary Hunt, founder of Debt-Proof Living, talking about her book *Raising Financially Confident Kids*, I knew we needed to make some changes. Mary is a hard-core budgeteer and financial planner. We are neither, but at the beginning of the summer, we began what I will call a light version experiment of her suggestions.

Mary's plan is somewhat different, but we based ours on her thoughts and then did what worked best for us. (You can find Mary's age-appropriate plans regarding kids and money in chapters 14–16 of her book.[1])

At the beginning of every month, we give our children a lump sum of money based on their age. We stagger the amount of money we give our kids from the youngest to the oldest. (A lump sum sounds way more than it is, but I think you have to figure out what will work for your family and budget.) Mary Hunt suggests monitoring what you spend on each child for a few months so you'll have a clear idea what the amount should be. It's more than you think it will be. We opted not to strictly follow that suggestion; instead we allotted our kids what we felt was enough for each of them without impacting our monthly budget.

We don't call the money we give our kids an allowance—it's considered a salary that they are earning for the work they do in the house.

We have chores in our house. My kids check the chart to see who is helping with dinner, who is cleaning up, and who is responsible for not letting our pets die from starvation, and we all pitch in on household and yard duties. This is expected and nonnegotiable. We don't call the money we give them an allowance—it's considered a salary that they are earning for the work they do in the house.

Terrell and I pay for all of their needs. And our kids use their salaries to pay for their wants.

Defining what "needs" are with your kids is an important conversation (and oh, so fun, when you are trying to convince your daughter she doesn't *need* every item on the hair aisle). At our house, items categorized as needs include a new pair of school shoes, new jeans if the old pair has worn out, haircuts, music lessons, etc. Needs are not the latest video game, toy, cute top at the mall, or newest gadget for my son's archery equipment.

This has rocked everyone's world—in a good way!

From watching one of my children spend every dime and then realize THAT WAS IT for the month to watching another save more than I thought possible, it's been a journey of education in teaching our children how to handle money.

Here's what I've learned from this experiment so far:

> It's easier for my kids to spend *my* money than *their* money.

> It has really made my children think before they spend. Numerous times I've watched them return something to the shelf after they realized they would need to use their own money to purchase it.

> It has reduced the proliferation of small "junk toys" that seem like such a tempting bargain.

> It's teaching them the value of a dollar.

> It's teaching them to save money. My son has way more money in his wallet than I do right now!

> It has significantly reduced the "gimmes" that were common on shopping trips.

> It's reminding them of the difference between wants and needs.

> It's teaching my kids about saving money for something they really want rather than spending it on immediate pleasures.

> It enforces the practice of not letting our kids borrow money from us.

> It has encouraged my kids to want to give money away to others. I love this! My son is dreaming of sponsoring his own child in a third-world country.

> It has my kids talking about opening their own savings accounts.

> It has made them more responsible. (Right off the bat, one of my kids lost their money in their room and it went missing for an entire month. That's one way to save!)

> This concept works amazingly well on trips and vacations too. We gave our kids a small amount of money when we went to the beach this summer. One blew the whole thing on a pricey shirt, one got a handful of trinkets, and one saved it. Everyone was happy and we stayed within our budget.

In *Raising Financially Confident Kids*, Hunt encourages the concept of giving 10 percent and saving 10 percent. Now that we've decided to incorporate the principles we established as a normal part of our home, we have added this concept.

3. We emphasize the value of hard work.

On the first day of summer in 1984, when Terrell was fourteen years old, his dad woke him up at seven o'clock to tell him that a load of sand had been delivered in the driveway and that by the time he got home from work, he expected all the low spots in the backyard to be filled. Oh, and a shovel was provided.

That's how my husband was raised.

Of course, Terrell's childhood wasn't all work and no play. He rode his bike all over town and played baseball, so I know he had fun, too. Still, there was a lot of hard work. For me growing up, we cleaned the house every Saturday without fail and then we did yard work, which included scooping dog poop. We didn't sleep until noon or play video games until the middle of the night while our mom fixed lunch and did all the laundry.

Last summer, we noticed a lot of grumbling when we asked our kids to help with the yard work or complete their chores, or even wake up before the entire morning was gone. Terrell and I talked about their attitudes and work ethic and decided to do something to get their attention. We know hard work not only teaches kids to be grateful for what you as a parent do all day long, it also creates a work ethic in them that will carry them into adulthood.

So yes, you guessed it, we had a load of sand delivered—and not just to make a point. Our kids knew about the uneven yard that held water. Sand was a good solution.

I wasn't prepared for all the bickering and whining. I knew our kids wouldn't love the idea, but *oh my.* Things got worse before they got better. Initially, my kids were very concerned about not outworking their siblings, so we devised a plan to make loading wheelbarrows, hauling sand, and spreading it as fair as possible. It was also a 100-degree day without any shade, so we accounted for the weather and had the kids work only an hour or two in the morning. With the first bleeding blister, I nearly caved. *Whose ridiculous idea was this anyway?*

Day after day, the kids worked, but they also argued and complained. At one point, I sat them down and said, "Yes, our yard needs this sand. Sure, we could have waited until we could pay someone to do it, but we've got fun stuff going on all summer—swimming and church camp and friends over. You will work together to complete this job without griping or I will have a second load delivered and we will do this all summer until you can learn to work as a team."

That little pep talk got the job more than halfway completed in near harmony, but a week later, we still had some sand in our driveway, even after the kids had each logged in many hours. Terrell and I joined them, and we all worked together on a Saturday to complete it. Everyone agreed it felt good to accomplish the huge task. My kids now refer to it proudly as the time they "fixed the backyard."

Here are some practical ways to teach kids how to work hard:

> Don't do everything for them: It sounds simple, but kids will *let* you do everything for them as long as you *do* everything for them.
> Require your kids to take care of their own spaces. They won't clean it up, you say? Try the age-old "You can't do or have (fill in the blank) until you clean up (fill in the blank)," and I bet they will.
> Make them sweat a little and literally get their hands dirty by picking up the trash in the street, washing the car, or scrubbing the trash can. It's okay. They will survive.
> Start early. Even very young ones can be given age-appropriate tasks.
> Make work part of your family routine. This is just something we do. We take care of what God has given us.
> Let them learn from their mistakes. Don't jump in to fix or redo everything they try to do. Let it go.
> Make work fun. We play chore roulette: Put all the chores in a jar and choose two. You create fun with a good attitude.
> Be an example of hard work. Let your kids see you working hard.
> Be an encourager rather than a control freak.

> Let your kids be in charge of dinner—from grocery shopping to putting it on the table. Last week I needed help so I asked my son to prepare dinner for the family. He had his doubts at first that he could handle everything, but he did a great job and ended up feeling as proud of himself as we did.
> Give them a chance to earn money so they can learn how to handle it.
> Teach them to save and give a percentage of their money.
> Give them projects that require time management skills (like a pile of sand on the driveway).
> Be consistent.

4. We teach responsibility and manage consequences.

Responsibility and consequences go hand in hand with the first two practical areas in this list. I think these are some of the hardest lessons to teach and let our kids learn. When Madison was in junior high, she caught up with me physically, meaning we could wear the same size in most things. She often asked to borrow sweaters and shoes and, well, everything. I had two simple rules: (1) Put it back where you got it when you're done, and (2) take care of it as if it were yours. There were times when she wasn't allowed to "shop" in my closet because she had broken one or the other of those rules.

One day, she borrowed a fabric headband and I told her to make sure she returned it at the end of the day because I was packing for a trip to Africa and headbands are my friends. When I didn't see the headband back in its place and asked her about it, Madison said, "Oh, it must be in my backpack." It wasn't. "Oh, it must be at school." Nope. It was gone.

I understand that things can get lost accidentally, but it was the response that "It only cost ten dollars" that I couldn't let pass.

Madi worked hard to make ten dollars to replace the headband. And she's never lost another one. It's not a surprise that kids are going to lose and break things. They are going to make mistakes and need second chances. But if we don't require something of them, they won't learn the lesson and they will keep making the same mistakes.

> *Kids are going to lose and break things, make mistakes and need second chances. But if we don't require something of them, they will keep making the same mistakes.*

There have been many occasions in this parenting journey when doling out consequences has been as painful for me as for my kids. As they have gotten older, they have earned more freedom and more responsibility. My teens are responsible for their laundry. I stopped nagging them about it, other than the occasional reminder that the washer and dryer are ready for their use. When they choose not to get their laundry done, they eventually run out of clothes to wear. We just keep quiet (this is very hard for me) because we know what's coming. "Dad, can I borrow some socks?" "Mom, can I get a shirt out of your closet?" We say no, and that usually results in unhappy kids.

But this is about much more than dirty laundry; it's about being responsible and following through with consequences. This exact scenario happened the other day, and we stood our ground. After Terrell and I shut our bedroom door, he said, "That went well." We both knew it didn't, but I understood what he meant. It was the right thing to do, even though it was really hard. We both believe the lightbulbs will turn on in our kids' minds one day and this simple lesson will become more deeply rooted.

In the meantime, it's hard watching our kids fail. But failure is often the best teacher. I've watched my teens ignore their piles of laundry, neglect their weekly chores, and basically give up easy money. When they reach a certain age and know what their responsibilities are, they don't need my constant reminding, and they know that if their weekly jobs aren't done by Sunday night, there isn't any money for the week. And by Wednesday or Thursday when they want to get a smoothie or a new shirt at the store, they remember the forgotten chores.

One of my kids received a generous amount of birthday money from friends and relatives and ended up using it in lieu of earning a salary over the course of a couple of months. It was hard to watch one of our kids choose not to complete the assigned chores, but it was an important lesson because guess what? Eventually that child of mine ran out of birthday money and started doing chores again, realizing there wasn't much left to show from the gifted money.

Kim is another one of our part-time Mercy House employees. She has raised four daughters and encourages me often by telling me that whatever phase or stage we are in is normal. (Advice to readers: You need an older or experienced mom in your life to regularly remind you of the same thing.) One day her daughter, who was a senior in high school at the time, texted Kim while she was working and asked her mom to bring her a school project that she had left at home. Kim replied, "No, I'm so sorry. But I reminded you last night while you were watching TV not to forget it." I thought of this story when I faced a similar situation with Jon-Avery and it solidified my resolve to let him manage the consequence of forgetting something he needed.

I was so encouraged by the lesson Kim was letting her daughter learn that day. Yes, it's hard for us not to jump in the car, rearrange our schedule, and bail our kids out. And sometimes we should. But when it becomes a habit or we want to see some responsibility in our kids, that's the last thing we should do.

Every school year as we are financially able, we give our kids a back-to-school allowance. It's always interesting to see how they spend their money. One year, one of my kids spent twice as much money as needed to buy a backpack that was in style. I knew that child wouldn't have enough money left for shoes and jeans, but I didn't nag. Sure enough, the funds ran out and the one with the fancy backpack had to live with the consequences. Another of our kids decided to keep using the same backpack purchased a couple of years earlier, in order to use the extra money to buy a second pair of new shoes. Letting our children develop responsibility and live with the consequences—good or bad—is a life lesson we need to give them.

5. We see the benefits of delayed gratification.

We've already mentioned our culture and its demand for instant gratification. Whatever we want, we want it right now. Our appetite for fast food has moved into every area of life, and we have the debt to prove it. As parents, we can delay gratification by making our kids wait for what they want. I love this definition of delayed gratification: It is *the ability to resist the temptation for an immediate reward and wait for a later reward.*[2]

The power of delayed gratification is best known from the Stanford Marshmallow Experiment, a study conducted by professor Walter Mischel at Stanford University. In this experiment, Mischel studied a group of four- to six-year-old children who were given a marshmallow and left in a room for fifteen minutes. These kids were given the choice to eat the marshmallow immediately or wait for fifteen minutes and be rewarded with a second marshmallow. Some waited, others didn't. Researchers continued to study the development of the children and learned that those who were able to wait, or delay gratification, were better adjusted, more motivated, and scored better grades in high school.[3]

When my kids work hard, save their money, and reach their goal of being able to buy something they really want, not only do they appreciate it more, they learn something in the delay. The reward is much sweeter.

Remember when I mentioned in chapter 4 how both of my daughters loved American Girl dolls? When Madison was eight years old, she really wanted Molly, one of the historical American Girl dolls. It wasn't our daughter's birthday and Christmas had already passed, and the truth was that we didn't have the money to get her what she wanted. I showed her secondhand Molly dolls on eBay for less than half the new price. Madison was determined. She started saving, and more important, she started working. Every day for weeks she asked for a job to do. We gave her a few, and then she approached her grandparents. She saved tooth fairy money, scrounged for quarters under the couch cushions, and did everything she could to get a few more coins toward her goal. After three months, she had what she needed. Other dolls have come and gone, now that Madison is old enough to drive, but Molly still sits on a shelf because the gratification of working for her isn't something Madison will forget. It made the prize even more special.

6. We give our kids a larger worldview.

Perspective is one of the most important gifts we can give our kids (and ourselves). And service is one of the best ways to package it. Kids are like us—their perspective is based on what is in front of them. As parents, I think it's our job to find ways to change how our children see the world by altering their view occasionally. If we see life through only one lens, we believe the misconception that everyone in the world has what we do, and our blessings start looking a lot like expectations. We can offer a new worldview in a variety of ways, but mostly it occurs through discomfort. What we know; where we live, work, attend school and church; what we eat—all these things are familiar and comfortable. It's not necessarily perfect or what we want, but we feel safe in what we know.

If we see life through only one lens, we believe the misconception that everyone in the world has what we do, and our blessings start looking a lot like expectations.

When I'm able to offer my kids a change in circumstances, I am always amazed at their reaction to being uncomfortable, touched by their compassion, and inspired by their motivation.

A year ago, early on a Saturday morning, we loaded up the car and drove an hour to a government housing complex. Twenty-two apartment buildings line either side of a long street, home to more than fifty thousand refugees relocated to our city.

A few of my friends, along with our husbands and kids, had joined The Refugee Project to help clean up the "clubhouse," where we help with a crocheting and knitting class for the refugee women. It was actually a vacant, musty three-bedroom apartment filled with an assortment of books, broken chairs, and dirty tables that needed a good scrubbing and fresh paint.

There was plenty of work to be done on this workday. We sorted and scrubbed and swept. We filled holes in the walls and stocked the shelves with books. We taped and painted, mopped, and dragged piles of trash bags to the dumpster.

Our children worked together to wrap more than six hundred crocheted bracelets onto cards that were going into the next Fair Trade Friday membership box. The cards had the word *Thrive* typed across them. That's the hope of The Refugee Project—that these displaced women will find a place in Christ and thrive.

I looked around the apartment and smiled at my family. Terrell, who hates to paint (at least that's what he tells me every time I ask), was completing a masterful job painting a wall. My son was wrapping bracelets, sitting next to my youngest, who was winding yarn into balls. My teen was in the bathroom creating face-paint designs on little children, with a long line of customers waiting their turns.

I stood in the center of that room and thought, *My children haven't complained once. They haven't asked for anything.* They didn't think of themselves while we worked hour after hour. They found a need and filled it. My next thought hit me so hard I had to blink back tears: *Our family is at its best—our absolute best—when we are doing something for someone else.*

When our hands are busy serving others, we aren't thinking about what we don't have. Instead, we are thankful for what we do have. We drove an hour away from our house to step into a different culture, and it broadened our worldview.

> When you love others, you complete what the law has been after all along. The law code—don't . . . always be wanting what you don't have, and any other "don't" you can think of—finally adds up to this: Love other people as well as you do yourself. You can't go wrong when you love others. When you add up everything in the law code, the sum total is *love*.
>
> ROMANS 13:8-10, MSG (italics in original)

It was after four in the afternoon when we piled back into the car and headed home. I was enjoying the comfortable quietness, realizing that the air was thick with satisfaction.

I turned back toward the kids. "Do you remember the sixteen-year-old refugee girl who helped us wrap bracelets?" They all nodded.

"She asked me if she could come to our class and learn to crochet like her sisters and mom and grandmother," I said. "Because she also wants to earn money."

"Doesn't she go to school?" Madison asked. I explained that she did, but she wanted the money for something special. "She plays the cello and is very talented. She earned a scholarship for a music school but still needs more money to make her dream a reality."

The car was quiet again, and I thought maybe my kids were thinking about how much they love music. Or maybe they were thinking about the instruments they own and love or the opportunity they have to take lessons. Or maybe they were wondering how to help a girl their age do the same.

"Mom," my twelve-year-old son broke the silence. "I loved today."

My heart nearly burst.

I think we were all created to ask the question, *What can I do that matters?* My job as a parent is to get my kids to ask it because when they do, they might just see the big world (and others) for the first time.

7. We strive to instill faithfulness.

We started off this chapter talking about consistency. Putting into practice what we want to be good at, what we believe in, who we want our families to be comes down to one word: faithfulness. I think this is almost a foreign concept in our culture—the tenacity to continue. The word *faithfulness* is defined with other words like *promise, vow, belief, duty, trust, reliability, loyalty.*

Today giving up is easy. If we don't like something, it's okay; we can always quit, especially if it gets hard or things don't go our way. At the sixth grade band concert, directors handed out awards to kids who had either performed exceptionally or met standards of excellence. Jon-Avery sat next to me, and I could tell he wanted his name to be called for percussion. He held his breath as the director got to his section and sighed when someone else was called. He mumbled something about it not being fair and about wanting to quit.

I leaned over and asked, "Why did that boy win?" Jon-Avery told me all the things his friend did right—from his practice ethic to achievement to behavior. We both knew that an area Jon-Avery needed to work on was talking too much. When he was done, I asked, "Do you do all those things?" He thought about it for a minute and said, "No, but I will."

I could tell this was important to him, and he was challenged to do better. By that time the following year, there was a marked difference in Jon-Avery's maturity, and before the second semester, he was moved to the top band and was one of only two seventh graders to make the all-district band.

Sometimes our kids want to quit because what they are doing isn't a good fit. Childhood is the perfect time to try out a lot of things. But many times, our kids quit because it's hard, and they lose out on the opportunity to learn. Our kids watched their dad go to a job every day for twelve years—one that provided for our family, one that Terrell didn't enjoy, one that was hard. This kind of faithfulness is difficult. Persevering when things aren't easy is often when we find our greatest reward.

I know on this parenting journey, there have been days when I've wanted to quit. The new phase was too uncertain, the fight too big, the hurt my child was experiencing too painful. On one particularly hard parenting day while writing this book, I told my husband, "Writing a book on parenting during a hard parenting day feels like writing a book on marriage while you're separated." Those days, I cried more than I wrote. But then I was reminded again that we were trying our best to first love God and then demonstrate His love to our kids and, as a family, to others around us.

I don't know where you are right now. You might be in any country in the world. You might be in the middle of your house, in the middle of suburbia folding laundry. You might be reading this on your shift break at your job in the hospital on the second floor. You might be standing in line at the pharmacy, waiting on medicine for your mother who is very sick. You might be in the lowest parenting season of your life or the best. I don't know. But it matters. Because you are where you are for a reason. Be faithful. You are living an example to your kids. You are showing them that when the going gets hard, you dig in your heels and you are faithful.

> *You are where you are for a reason. Be faithful. You are living an example to your kids.*

Because maybe there's someone in your world, at your job, in your neighborhood, on your path who needs to know that you are where you are because you can help that person where he or she is. Someone is waiting for you to share your money, your time, and your life.

GOING AGAINST THE FLOW

Parents

> It's easy to get overwhelmed by all we need to teach our kids. Start slow and make it manageable for everyone. Be encouraged that what you're doing matters.

Toddlers/Preschoolers

> Start chores early. The earlier kids learn that hard work yields positive results, the easier it gets.
> Consistency is one of the greatest gifts we can give our younger kids. Create room in your family schedule to serve regularly and work together.

Elementary

> Create a separate job jar (aside from regular chores). When your kids ask for something, offer a chance to earn it first.
> Look for practical ways to broaden their worldview, such as cooking recipes from other countries, serving different people groups, and so forth.

Tweens/Teens

> Give your kids an economic challenge or goal to work toward. We've told our kids we will match dollar for dollar whatever they can save toward a car. One of them is saving like crazy, the other not so much. One will probably drive before the other.
> Create opportunities for your tweens and teens to take ownership. Give them a budget, let them plan, invite them to be a part of something that involves the entire family—their responsibility might just surprise you.

CHAPTER 10

DEAR PARENTS

THE FOLLOWING PAGES ARE probably the most important in this book, and yet they might be the hardest to read. We've made it to the last chapter, and it could be different from what you were expecting. Most books wrap everything up in a tidy package. But I can't tie up these chapters neatly with a bow because parenting is messy. Oh, it's also wonderful and the highest calling of our lives, but it's probably one of the hardest things we will ever do.

Here's what you must know: If you go against the cultural flow and lead your family upstream, doing the things I've suggested, it's completely possible that all hell will break loose in your home. Even with a big bow on it, that's a difficult truth to swallow.

RAISING GRATEFUL KIDS IN AN ENTITLED WORLD

You might have a child who embraces your parenting wholeheartedly. And you might have one who fights you every step of the way. I have experienced both responses.

Think about how hard it is for us as adults to go against what everyone is doing. Human nature makes us want to be like everyone else, to do what is popular and culturally acceptable. And when we don't, we often become the target, or at the very least, feel left out and alone. There have been many occasions when I have put my kids in a hard place by what I've asked them to do or by the way we've chosen to live as a family.

It started when they were young, when I thought the change would be seemingly harmless. We made a decision as a family—before our oldest started school—not to allow our kids to spend the night with families we didn't know well. When Madison got that first invitation to a party that all her kindergarten friends were going to, it upset her that she couldn't go, and she cried all afternoon about it. When my kids were young, I would say, "Just blame me. Tell your friends it was your mom's choice," to try to ease the burden of feeling left out. But that only works so long. Through the years, we stuck by our choice and only allowed them sleepovers with close family friends or family because it was the right choice for us, even if it went against what other parents decided. The result is that my kids have turned down many invitations.

When my girls started caring about clothes and fashion, we constantly had to make decisions that were hard for them. And even though we've spent years teaching them about modesty, we face a new challenge nearly every season. It's not easy finding shorts for our daughters that cover more than their rear ends—and barely that much. And it's not easy being the only fifteen-year-old at the pool not wearing a bikini. I'm not saying that it's sinful to do either, but Terrell and I decided it's not right for our daughters, even if they are the only ones dressed differently. As they have gotten older, I've been able to share more of the why behind our convictions. My teenager understands what lust is and how visually stimulated boys are, but sometimes she still asks because she wants to wear what everyone else is wearing.

Here's the simple truth that isn't so simple: Raising kids to be different from the world really does make them different from the world.

Here's the simple truth that isn't so simple: Raising kids to be different from the world really does make them different from the world. This is true whether you homeschool them or send your kids to public or private school. Once you set them on that path, they will stand out when all they want to do is blend in. Teachers and other parents will probably notice, but kids will immediately zero in on this. My children have been praised by other adults, teachers, and even childless couples for being different from other kids. But they have struggled with feeling left out and mentioned often that they feel weird. They are warm, friendly kids and hardly social outcasts, but they do notice when they aren't invited or included in invitations to activities or events. Being different is as hard now as it was when we were kids. I've heard Terrell share the story with our kids about not going to his senior prom or any of the high school dances because he wanted to be different, but then being given a hard time by his friends who attended.

Every family has to deal with specific issues—such as allowing kids to be dropped off at the mall for the day without adult supervision or letting them date at a young age, both of which we don't support—but when you decide to push against a cultural norm, there will be people in your life and community, even your church, who will question you. Amazingly, we've experienced the most criticism from other Christian parents. I think it's because our refusal to do what others are doing makes them question what they are doing.

And you must know, there have been tense friction and terrible fights, tears and tantrums on this journey. We know we are asking our kids to do hard things. I love the quote from Alex and Brett Harris's book *Do Hard Things: A Teenage Rebellion against Low Expectations*, which we read as a family. "Our uprising is against a cultural mind-set that twists the purpose and potential of the teen years and threatens to cripple our generation. Our uprising won't be marked by mass riots and violence, but by millions of individual teens quietly choosing to turn the low expectations of our culture upside down."[1] If we expect our kids to give in, they might. But if we expect them to be different, to make hard choices, they might surprise us.

Giving kids a world perspective reminds them that even though being different in our society can be challenging, it's not usually life-threatening.

I think this is why giving our kids a world perspective is so important. It doesn't make their day-to-day peer pressure less, but it reminds them that even though being different in our society can be challenging, it's not usually life-threatening like it is in many places around the world. It's not the kind of persecution that puts their lives at risk or places them in desperate situations where they have to make unthinkable decisions to survive.

The bottom line is this: All the right-from-wrong-teaching, character-building, faith-instilling, intentional parenting that you've made a priority in your home is producing children who do not fit into the mold our society has deemed normal. And it leaves us with children who sometimes feel left out, different, alienated, and even alone. But this doesn't mean we've failed them. It's through this kind of struggle that their own faith is forged and deepens and their relationship with us—bumpy days included—grows. But mostly, it makes them aware of the costs of following Jesus.

When Jon-Avery was in junior high, he went on a weekend trip with our church and stayed overnight with boys his age. He had looked forward to the trip, but when he chose not to join in some questionable conversations, he felt like the odd man out. He didn't tell any of the adults at the time because he didn't want to be pegged as a tattletale. Later when I picked him up, I could tell something was wrong. He was withdrawn and quiet and didn't seem excited about the weekend he had just had.

Once we were alone, I sat on the couch with my son, and as he described the situation and how it made him feel and how he responded, I cried. I hugged him as I said, "I am so proud of you. You are a brave kid. It's not easy standing up when it means standing alone." I would have given anything to protect my son from ever feeling that way again, but I can't because I'm partially to blame. We've raised him to be kind to others, to avoid coarse language, to follow Jesus no matter the cost.

There will be growing pains raising grateful kids upstream in a downstream world of entitlement.

It will make our kids feel different.

It will get harder before it gets easier.

It will make them feel alone.

It might make you doubt the course.

It will probably cause fights and friction.

Who's ready to sign up?

Terrell sometimes says I'm a pessimist. I argue that I'm actually a realist because I want you to know the cost up front. Even with all of the challenges, I wouldn't change this journey. I can see glimpses of hope and promise when I see my kids live out their faith. I can see my kids put others first when it's not natural to do so. I can see gratitude shaping who they are becoming.

ESSENTIAL CONVERSATIONS

We have a beautiful opportunity to walk beside our children in their own journeys. It's a privilege. And we can help them. As we are teaching and following through on the truths we've discussed in this book, we can also be their greatest encouragers.

When we were working as a family to memorize Psalm 23, we took turns quoting the verses in different voices to make it fun. (I've discovered that you do what works to keep everyone engaged. In this instance, Terrell was doing a redneck accent.) Once everyone had memorized the passage after a few weeks, we wrote it from memory. And then we took some time to talk about what it meant.

When we got to verse 4, "your rod and your staff protect

and comfort me," I talked to the kids about David's job tending sheep. "Do you know what the staff was for?" I asked.

"It was used to direct the sheep, to pull them back from the edge of danger and make them go a certain way," Madison replied.

"That's right. But what about the rod?" I asked.

"That's what the shepherd would use to discipline them," Jon-Avery said. "Womp!" We laughed as he thunked an imaginary sheep on the head.

"Why do you think David said that these things comforted him? Who is comforted by being disciplined?"

I think my kids knew where I was going because Emerson said, "The shepherd loves the sheep."

"Yes, that's right," Terrell brought the point home. "Just like Mom and I do with you. We correct you because we love you. And even if it doesn't feel comforting, imagine life without it."

If you're like me, attempting to navigate this course with God's help, here are four essential conversations we need to have with our children that we can start when they are young and continue to have with them until they leave home.

1. *It's okay to be different.* I'll never forget when Jon-Avery was in the fourth grade. He came home one day, stood in the kitchen, and delivered this verbal blow: "I'm the weird one, Mom."

I grabbed his hand, the one with marker stains and chewed fingernails, and refuted his words. "There's nothing weird about you!"

Then he opened up his heart, admitting how different he felt from most of the other boys his age at school who were using cuss words and bullying other students in an effort to look tough. Jon-Avery has always been sensitive, but before I could chalk it up to his tender personality, he said, "It's hard being a Christian. It makes me odd."

I felt my own tears press hot against my lids. I closed my eyes and remembered the feeling of alienation, the one I lived with growing up. I couldn't discount my son's words or his pain; I knew they were true. He just seemed so young to feel them.

"Were you ever the weird one, Mom?"

I told him my own stories, many of which I included in my book *Rhinestone Jesus*, the title inspired by the sparkly Jesus pin I wore in high school. "I put the *w* in weird, honey." We laughed, and I whispered words of encouragement and prayed. I reminded him that we are called to be the strangers of this world, to follow a narrow road, to live in a way that's countercultural.

I think it's important to include grace in this conversation for the times our kids end up making a wrong choice or following the crowd. "We don't expect you to be perfect, Jon-Avery. We know there will be pressure to give in, but we all learn from our mistakes. And we'll love you no matter what."

His response struck a deep chord in me that day. "I know I can fit in. I just don't want to." It's been more than five years since that conversation. There have been failures along the way. But he knows in his heart that although being different is hard, it's also okay.

2. *I'm sorry.* Terrell and I have made countless mistakes in this parenting journey. We've been too strict when we

should have offered grace. We've been too lenient when we should have given consequences. We have blundered and we have hurt our kids. Even unintentional pain is still pain. Apologizing is a critical part of good parenting. And sometimes the best way to teach our kids how to apologize is to lead by example. I tend to talk too much, and I'm really good at telling my kids what to do. As they've gotten older, I've realized they know how I feel on almost every subject, and there comes a time when I just need to hush and listen. Recently, Jon-Avery asked me to do just that concerning an issue with his sister. I wanted him to apologize, and he just needed me to give him space to take care of it in his way. I realized he was right, and I took a dose of my own advice and offered him an apology instead.

We don't have to apologize for the why as much as the how. I'm not sorry for wanting grateful kids instead of entitled ones. I am not sorry for believing in and teaching my kids absolute truth. But I am sorry for how I go about it at times, how controlling I can be, how my words wound.

3. *I don't always understand but I want to try.* "You just don't understand!" I've heard these words said in frustration and anguish by my kids on more than one occasion. And my temptation is to respond, "Yes, I do. I understand." But if I'm honest with myself, even though we can empathize with our kids, we aren't walking in their shoes. We can't imagine how times have changed since we were their age. We don't understand the pressure to conform or give in. I remember the first time I didn't give that pat answer to Madison. We were in a heated discussion about her responsibility to manage her

There will be times we simply don't understand what our kids are going through. But that doesn't mean we are unable to help them. Any attempt goes a long way.

time and keep up with her chores in the middle of a very hectic marching band season. "Mom, you have no idea," she said. "You just don't understand."

My automatic response was on the tip of my tongue but I said, "You're right. Help me understand. I want to try." We had a great conversation, and I ended up understanding more of the pressure she was feeling. Instead of telling her again to clean up her room, I helped her.

There will be times we simply don't understand what our kids are going through. But that doesn't mean we are unable to help them. Any attempt goes a long way.

4. *You are not alone.* These four words are the most important ones we can say to our kids, from the first time they experience toddler separation anxiety until we move them into their first apartment. We all know that at some point in their lives they will, in fact, be physically alone. Being alone isn't a bad thing, but it can be scary, especially for young kids. When we drop them off at preschool, we whisper in their ears, "It's okay. I will be back. I promise," and then high-five the other moms in the parking lot. We know this kind of "being alone from us occasionally" is a good thing. But when they struggle with being alone, it is the perfect opportunity to introduce the truth that Jesus always is with them, so they understand that even in times of separation from us, they are never truly alone.

As our kids grow, most of them seem to want time away from us. What they are actually looking for is space. They don't want us to leave them completely alone, even when they are seventeen, slam their door, and scream, "Leave me alone!" This is when our kids especially need to hear these words because they are probably feeling vulnerable and as if they are the only ones in the world facing their present struggles. We can hold fast to the promise in Deuteronomy 31:6 that we should remind our kids—and ourselves—often: "Be strong and courageous. Do not fear or be in dread of them, for it is the LORD your God who goes with you. He will not leave you or forsake you" (ESV).

We can say to our kids: Not only is God with you, we are too—our family—you, me, us. We are a team and we will journey this road, navigate the bumps, and overcome the obstacles together.

SO WHAT CAN WE DO?

I don't think there are boxes to check or a specific formula to adhere to in parenting other than following Christ and leading our kids to do the same by faithful, godly living. After that, the choice to continue on that path is ultimately up to our kids to make. We lead them to the place where they have everything they need to make it. I love this comment left on my parenting poll by someone who was looking back on her own parenting, "My husband and I are in awe of the children we have raised. We joke that we only know we did three things right: Our kids knew (1) we loved God, (2) we loved each other, and (3) we loved them!"

I believe we can help our kids learn to choose wisely by making the following actions a priority for them and for us as parents.

We Can Choose to Live in Christian Community

Nothing has helped our family more on this countercultural road than living in community with families who have the same goals. No, we haven't moved to a religious compound or formed an exclusive clique. But we intentionally spend time with people who want the same results we do. That doesn't mean it's perfect or even tidy. When we let people into our lives and become vulnerable, they are going to see our mess. They will know we don't have it all together; they will see that we are just like them.

When Jon-Avery got into a misunderstanding with one of his friends in our community, the boys tried to work it out on their own, but then we parents got involved. It was awkward and uncomfortable because both of our sons had made mistakes, and it caused momentary tension between the families. But thankfully, it wasn't too long before my friend said, "Hey, let's talk through all of this because our kids are going to grow up together, we are doing life with your family, and we will be stronger if we face the ugly parts together."

Most of my kids' education has been in public school (we reevaluate every year and choose what's best for each kid). Connecting with believers their age has always been a very high priority for our family. This commitment has been lifesaving in many ways because it has given them positive peer influence in every season. They have connected with other Christian kids at school, but their primary community has been at church or in youth group. It always makes me sad when I hear about parents grounding their kids from church activities for some infraction. Our kids need this community. They probably also need a consequence for whatever they are in trouble for, but I think we should choose something that isn't a part of their spiritual growth and connection.

We Can Make Our Home a Safe Place

"I hope you don't act this way at school!" Raise your hand if you've said it. I have. I used to wonder why my kids would get glowing reports at school, church, and extracurricular activities, and then come home and act like little devils. An older mom once cleared it up for me. "Kristen, isn't this what you want? You teach them how to act and treat others, and they are doing it where it's most

> *I want my home to be a safe place. I want my kids to feel secure enough to confess their struggles and sin and share their successes.*

important. They conform to society's rules of no touching or talking in the hallway, and when they get home, they just need to let it all out. They feel safe at home—that's why you see them at their worst." Well, let me tell you, that was good news for this mom. That's not to say from that moment on, it was a free-for-all at home. We kept the same structure and rules as we always had, but it helped me understand the difference in the two environments.

I want my home to be a safe place. I want it to be the place they bring their friends and hang out. I want my kids to feel secure enough to confess their struggles and sin and share their successes.

We Can Choose Relationship over Rules

Terrell and I both grew up in a legalistic denomination. We constantly worried about losing our salvation, and this kind of atmosphere makes rules pretty important. Although we're trying to raise our kids in a grace-filled home, sometimes old habits die hard. My nature is to follow rules. It took me a long time to see that rule-following doesn't always reflect a heart for doing what's right. We all know people who hold hard and fast to a rule that says "this sin is wrong" while they make other choices that might be worse. When we choose grace over legalism, we are really choosing relationship over rules.

That's not to say we shouldn't have rules. I have a long list. But there must be flexibility, too. There will be times when we have to lay aside our rules to save the relationship. For example, early on I made the rule that everyone had to eat everything on their dinner plates every night or else face consequences. I tried to enforce it, but one of my kids has struggled for years with sensory reactions to certain food textures that makes doing what I've asked a consistent battle. So instead, I avoid the couple of foods that trigger this kid's issues and, as a rule, I ask the sensitive eater to try whatever is served because "you just might like it." And if this kid doesn't, there is always peanut butter and bread available; I'm not fixing two dinners. (Some of you die-hard "sit there until your dinner is gone, and if you don't eat it, you're having it for breakfast" people are cringing right now, I'm sure.) But we've found something that works for us, because my way was actually making dinner a nightmare for our family, and it was hurting my relationship with my child.

When our kids push against us, our first reaction is to push back. But many times when they are struggling, they don't need more discipline—they need more love. When one of my kids is rude and disrespectful, my first reaction is to be rude and disrespectful back. (I wonder where they get that from?) My second reaction is to offer a punishment. But when I lay aside my rules and take them out for coffee, or deflate their anger by apologizing first, they often open up and let me into their world, and then I can get at the root of the problem. Wisdom is one of the greatest gifts we can ask God for.

> *When our kids push against us, our first reaction is to push back. But many times when they are struggling, they don't need more discipline—they need more love.*

We Can Pray for Our Children

This last point is the most important. Nothing we do or say can ever substitute for bowing our heads and praying for our children. There have been some really hard days in this journey when I've gone to bed burdened for one of my kids and slept fitfully, only to face another conflict the next morning. Thankfully, this has been seasonal and not always ongoing, but it wears me out and sometimes makes me feel like a failure. I have wanted to give up many times. And I have found comfort and peace in only one place—on my knees. There is something deeply spiritual and healing about humbling our bodies and our pride and laying the burden at Jesus' feet.

I have a prayer list on my phone, and I try to pray through

it several times a week, lifting up those in our lives who are oppressed, sick, and discouraged and praying over the hard work God has asked us to oversee. All of my kids are listed with requests next to their names. "God, give Jon-Avery a good Christian friend at school." "Please help Emerson to control her anger with her brother and sister." "Be with Madison during these last years of high school. Help her to know how deeply she is loved by You."

As a mom, nothing makes me feel less alone or more encouraged than giving my parenting burdens to the One who parents me.

Prayer is often the last thing we think of when it comes to difficult parenting days. We reserve it for our desperate moments, when there's an unexpected diagnosis or rebellion. But God wants to walk this path with us. As a mom, nothing makes me feel less alone or more encouraged than giving my parenting burdens to the One who parents me.

THE KEY TO RAISING GRATEFUL KIDS

One particular question on my parenting poll garnered the identical answer from nearly all of the respondents: What do you think the key is to raising grateful kids? *We raise grateful kids by modeling gratitude.*

We teach gratitude by living it. We are the example. Ah, it sounds so simple.

Looking back to my own parents' example, I have mental snapshots of my dad in his old blue bathrobe, on his knees crying onto his worn Bible, praying for me in the early morning hours, thanking God for his life and his family. I watched my parents empty their savings account and give it to people in need because they were grateful for the abundance they had received. For years, I listened to my dad talk about and pray over a small Muslim country (one he has never visited) because God told him to. That small country's flag hung in our church as a visual reminder to pray for the oppressed people group it represented, and it was a way of broadening my worldview. My parents modeled gratitude, and there's no doubt that my love for the poor women of the world and any generosity I possess was birthed in this snapshot.

I would love for my kids to say one day they are grateful for their lives because their dad and I were grateful for ours. I want them to have memories of me thanking God for all He's done. I want them to catch me writing thank-you notes and being generous with my time and money because God has been generous with me. But most of all, I want my children to know that we wanted them to resist the current of our culture and choose a lifestyle of gratitude because we love them deeply and completely.

I want my children to know that we wanted them to choose a lifestyle of gratitude because we love them deeply.

Last summer, when our kids left for camp, Terrell and I were devastated at the five days alone, so we sulked all the way to San Antonio for a little rest and relaxation. While we were there, we got a text midweek from our pastor, who had visited the camp that day. It read, "Your kids are rock stars. They are super servants. I'm at camp today, and I have watched them in action, and everything you've worked for and care about as parents is evidenced today in the way they love and serve others."

I couldn't stop the tears. I was so grateful that our pastor took the time to bless us with those words. I was so grateful to God for the gift of perspective. Sometimes we are so close to our kids that we can't see who they are becoming, and we need others to remind us of what they see. It was the first time I actually felt like I should be writing this book. Of course, a couple of days later, we picked up some dirty and exhausted children and had a big fat family fight over tacos again for dinner. But I still cherish those words from our pastor today.

Gratitude in our convenient, gratification-filled, selfie-obsessed, entitled society is a rarity. Choosing to lead our families against the flow of our culture will cost us. David Platt points out in *Counter Culture* that Luke 9:23 sums up what it means to follow Christ.

If anyone would come after me, let him deny himself and take up his cross daily and follow me. (ESV)

Platt puts it into a present-day perspective. "Talk about countercultural. In a world where everything revolves around yourself—protect yourself, promote yourself, comfort yourself, and take care of yourself—Jesus says, 'Crucify yourself. Put aside all self-preservation in order to live for God's glorification, no matter what that means for you in the culture around you.'"[2]

Our kids are watching us. And when we feel like we are failing or we don't know what to do next, the answer is always to get closer to Jesus because when we do, those around us might just inch closer too.

I love the way *The Message* translates 1 John 2:15-17:

Don't love the world's ways. Don't love the world's goods. Love of the world squeezes out love for the Father. Practically everything that goes on in the world—wanting your own way, wanting everything for yourself, wanting to appear important—has nothing to do with the Father. It just isolates you from him. The world and all its wanting, wanting, wanting is on the way out—but whoever does what God wants is set for eternity.

So grab your paddle, friends. This parenting course is beautiful and turbulent. There will be days you will long for the final destination of watching your children enter adulthood. But often the real joy is the journey of *getting there.*

ACKNOWLEDGMENTS

Terrell: More than anyone, you know how difficult this book was to write—and more, how challenging it's been to live. Thank you for encouraging me every step of the way, for doing hard things, for leading our home so well. You are an amazing dad and the perfect husband for me. I love you with every breath.

Madison: I begged God to make me a mother and He gave me *you*. There hasn't been a day since that you haven't taught me something about life and about myself. You are brave and strong and the loveliest world changer I know. I love you, honey.

Jon-Avery: Your quiet nature, compassionate heart for others, and steadfastness have ministered to my momma's heart longer than you can know. I thank God for you and I cannot wait to see how you change the world. I love you, son.

Emerson: Your little life is a whisper of God's daily grace in our home. You are determined and fierce and you keep me on my toes. I love watching you grow, and I'm convinced your mark on the world will be known. I love you, baby.

Maureen: You're my daughter by way of the Cross, and I love you. Watching you become a mother, and thus making me a *shosh* (Kenyan grandmother), has been pure joy. I hope this book helps you someday.

To the daughters of Kenya: You've wound your way into my heart, and it's an honor serving you. Every time you call me "Mom Kristen" I am humbled by the mothers you've become. Even though oceans separate us, God connects us.

Mom: Thank you for always being there for me. There has never been a moment or day that I needed you and you didn't rush to help or heal. During some of my challenging parenting moments, I've drawn strength from knowing that one day I will be friends with my kids. Thanks for giving me that hope. I love you.

Dad: If there is anything good or grateful in me, you probably had a lot to do with it. Parenting these kids has given me a lot of aha moments regarding how you raised me. So I should probably say I'm sorry for all those eye rolls and slammed doors. I've always been a Daddy's girl. Thanks for giving me a reason to keep coming home. I love you.

To Bud and Betty: Thank you for raising your son to be grateful. You did a great job and because of it, our family is thankful. I love you and couldn't ask for better in-laws.

Kara: I love you, sister. I'm so thankful for your friendship and that we are figuring this all out together.

To the readers of *We Are THAT Family* and my blogging friends: This book exists because of you. Thank you for giving me a safe place to write about my parenting struggles—the good, the bad, and the ugly. Thank you for sharing my parenting posts, encouraging me along the way, and saying yes with me for so long!

To my agent, Bill Jensen: Bill, you championed the idea of this book and held my hand a lot during its development. Thank you. You're an amazing dad, and you give great advice.

To my dearest friends: Suzanne—for listening to me complain and suggesting new topics for this book regularly; Jessica—for being my neighbor and parenting-fallback girl; Kim—for telling me, *This is normal*; Taylor—for reminding me of the new joys of motherhood; and Tracy—for comparing our strong-willed daughters and making me feel better.

To my house church: I love you guys. Thanks for praying me through this book.

To Trace and Lee Howard: Thank you for helping me to rightly divide Scripture and for encouraging me as this manuscript became a reality.

To my fellow (in)Courage writers: Y'all know what this whole process feels like, and I'm so thankful that I have sisters to lean on through it.

To the Tyndale Momentum publishing team: Sarah, for believing in this book and validating me as an author, making me feel that what I have to say might help someone step closer to God; Bonne, for lovingly turning me into a wordsmith; Sharon, for coming all the way to Houston to learn more about our family's yes to God; Cassidy, for not saying no when I threw outlandish ideas at you and everyone else for making this book possible.

To Jesus: Thank you for making me a mom. It's been the hardest and most fulfilling yes of my life, and I'm so grateful I'm doing it with Your help.

APPENDIX A

CELL PHONE CONTRACT BETWEEN PARENT AND CHILD

I will not text or place phone calls after 9 p.m.

I will plug my phone in downstairs by 9 p.m.

I will not bring my cell phone to the family dinner table.

I will not send threatening or mean texts to others.

I will babysit my little sister in exchange for my basic phone bill to be paid.

I will not go over our plan's monthly minutes or text message limits. If I do, I understand that I may be responsible for paying any additional charges or that I may lose my cell phone privileges.

I understand that I am responsible for knowing where my phone is and for keeping it in good condition.

I understand that my cell phone may be taken away as a consequence of disrespect and breaking this contract.

I will use phone etiquette in public places (like not using it at dinner or walking and texting). I will make sure it is turned off when I am in church or other quiet settings.

I will obey any rules my school has regarding cell phones.

I promise I will alert my parents when I receive alarming phone calls or text messages from people I know or don't know.

I will also alert my parents if I am being harassed by someone via my cell phone.

I will not send embarrassing photos of my family or friends to others.

I understand that having a cell phone is a privilege.

CHRISTIAN PARENT MANIFESTO

This world is not our final home.

Because of this, we won't always fit in, and actually, we should strive not to conform to the world.

The Bible is our standard for holiness and guides our everyday living.

Truth may shift in our culture, but we look to God's Word as our standard.

There will be people who choose to live differently than we do. This doesn't affect, change, or alter how we treat them.

We love people no matter what.

There are scary things in this world, but we can hold fast to the peace of God.

His peace comforts us when we don't understand things around us.

God is in control, and He sees all and knows all.

One day, He will return for us. This is our blessed hope.

Until that day, we will stand for what we believe is right.

We will serve others who cannot serve themselves.

We will speak up for those who have been muffled by oppression and poverty.

We will give more than we take.

We will love others because He first loved us.

We will follow Jesus.

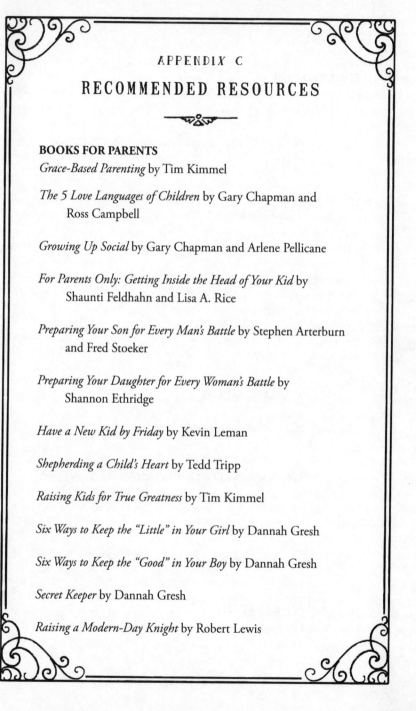

RECOMMENDED RESOURCES

BOOKS FOR PARENTS

Grace-Based Parenting by Tim Kimmel

The 5 Love Languages of Children by Gary Chapman and Ross Campbell

Growing Up Social by Gary Chapman and Arlene Pellicane

For Parents Only: Getting Inside the Head of Your Kid by Shaunti Feldhahn and Lisa A. Rice

Preparing Your Son for Every Man's Battle by Stephen Arterburn and Fred Stoeker

Preparing Your Daughter for Every Woman's Battle by Shannon Ethridge

Have a New Kid by Friday by Kevin Leman

Shepherding a Child's Heart by Tedd Tripp

Raising Kids for True Greatness by Tim Kimmel

Six Ways to Keep the "Little" in Your Girl by Dannah Gresh

Six Ways to Keep the "Good" in Your Boy by Dannah Gresh

Secret Keeper by Dannah Gresh

Raising a Modern-Day Knight by Robert Lewis

BOOKS FOR TEENS

Do Hard Things: A Teenage Rebellion against Low Expectations by Alex and Brett Harris

Start Here: Doing Hard Things Right Where You Are by Alex and Brett Harris

You Were Made to Make a Difference by Max Lucado and Jenna Lucado Bishop

Make Every Day Count (teen edition) by Max Lucado

Jesus Freaks: Martyrs: Stories of Those Who Stood for Jesus by DC Talk

The Hiding Place by Corrie ten Boom

Running for My Life by Lopez Lomong

Kisses from Katie by Katie Davis

The Body Book by Nancy Rue (preteen)

ONLINE SITES (FOR INTERNET FILTERING)

Net Nanny: www.netnanny.com

Safe Eyes: www.internetsafety.com

Covenant Eyes: http://www.covenanteyes.com

EXPERIENCE WEEKEND

Family Life Passport2Purity: www.familylife.com/passport2purity

DISCUSSION GUIDE

This study guide for *Raising Grateful Kids in an Entitled World* will help you go deeper in personally applying the message of how to cultivate gratitude in your kids. Invite others to join you—your spouse, other parents, or a church group—or use this guide on your own for individual reflection. While it is structured as a four-week study, feel free to adapt it for a shorter or longer time to suit your needs. For more resources, visit www.raisinggratefulkids.com.

WEEK 1: INTRODUCTION AND LAUNCH
Introduction

1. What made the cowboy boot incident so impactful for Kristen? What did she learn about herself and her child? What do you think the child learned?

2. What memories of hard work do you have from your own childhood? What qualities do these memories reveal about yourself, your family's priorities, and the way your personal work ethic developed?

3. Would you agree with Kristen that our culture is "obsessed" with happiness? How so? What elements of wanting your children to be happy do you consider positive or negative?

4. How do you see God working in your family? How do you think faith might guide your choices as you seek to cultivate a spirit of gratitude in your home?

5. Kristen reminds us that "anytime we step out of the mainstream and try to turn our lives (or homes) around and dare to go upstream, it's hard." What challenges do you face as a parent as you try to cultivate a more grateful family? What hopes, goals, and promises will you keep in mind to encourage yourself to hang in there when it gets tough?

Chapter 1: Wants vs. Needs

1. How would you complete the sentence: "What I want most for my kids is _____"?

2. Kristen confesses a time when she wanted something she couldn't yet have. Can you relate? What are some of your own personal wants? How are they different from your needs?

3. Think of a time when you as a child were truly grateful for a gift or a special event, or when your hard work earned a reward or a compliment. What happened and how did it make you feel? Is there a way that experience has influenced you as a parent?

4. What do your kids own (iPods, toys, computers) that are beyond what you had at their age? How do you see these possessions influencing your kids, for better or for worse?

Chapter 2: Times Have Certainly Changed

1. We can't ultimately control everything our kids are exposed to as they're growing up. Have you ever felt in over your head when your kids ask about something questionable they've seen on the news or in magazines, or heard in school? How do you respond?

2. "I knew if we allowed [our daughter] to struggle with her questions and gave her freedom to ask them, she would become stronger in her beliefs in the end," Kristen says. Why was she initially afraid for her daughter to ask the hard questions? What is a question you and your family have struggled with, and what have you learned about each other as you've worked through it?

3. "God often uses mistakes, wayward choices, and brokenness to bring redemption." How have you seen this to be true in your own family? Do you find it difficult to trust that it would be true for your children too?

WEEK 2: UNDERTOW
Chapter 3: Seven Ways We Parents Miss the Boat (and How to Get on Board)

1. What do you think of the comment that kids "don't question that they will receive a smartphone or a car someday; they believe it is a right of childhood"? Have you seen that to be true in your own community? Do you

believe that any "rights of childhood" exist, and if so, what are they? How might your kids answer the same question?

2. Which of the "things parents do [that] they know they shouldn't" in this chapter do you resonate with most? What are some of the reasons you have said no to your kids' "wants"? What was the result?

3. Describe a time when "fitting in" seemed to be all that mattered to you or your kids. What does it mean to you to "fit in?" Why do you think it is so important to us? What are some things you would say are even more important and why?

4. Although it is so hard to see our children struggle, what might they lose long-term by always being rescued and never experiencing failure or setbacks? Think of some of your own best character qualities—perhaps they include kindness, resilience, patience, or humor. How were those qualities shaped or formed partly by the hard times in your life?

Chapter 4: The Selfie Society

1. Describe a time when you felt special because you sensed your parents were truly proud of you. Then think of a time when you felt proud in the same way about your own child's character or decisions. Do the two experiences have anything in common?

2. What is something you do even though you may not be the best at it? What do you love about it? What do you hope your kids learn from watching you do it?

3. What does it mean to you to have a "child-centered home"? How have Kristen's opinions on this topic changed and why, and what happened in her family as a result? What would you say is at the center of your own home?

Chapter 5: Making Smart Choices about Technology

1. How much access do your own kids have to technology? Is it different from what their peers have? What platform would you say is most important to your kids (TV, smartphone, computer, social media) and how do you feel about the amount of time they spend on it?

2. How can you be proactive in this area as your kids continue to grow?

3. Why do you think Kristen says that the most important thing we can teach our kids is self-control?

WEEK 3: RESISTING THE CURRENT
Chapter 6: Cultivating Obedience

1. Kristen believes that once we decide on and communicate a consequence to our kids, we do more harm than good if we back down. Have you found this to be true in your own family? What are some of the hardest things about standing firm? What are the benefits to doing it anyway? Are there any risks or pitfalls?

2. How does your love and care for your children help you to better understand God's love and care for us?

3. How do you teach your kids about money? How do you approach allowances, paying for chores, and instructing

your kids in saving and spending? Do you see any ways you could use such moments to intentionally instill values like hard work and sacrifice?

4. Do you agree with the statement: "It's okay for our kids not to be rewarded all the time"? Why or why not?

Chapter 7: Living Out God's Love in Your Home

1. "Checking church off the list," Kristen says, "or having a Christian channel as a radio preset, or hanging a cross in our home doesn't make us followers of Jesus." How would you define a follower of Jesus? How does faith play a role in your family life?

2. "Parents say much more to their kids by their lives than by their words." What do you see your life saying to your children?

3. Describe a time when you let a child make his or her own choice about whether to participate in an activity. What happened? How did you and the child ultimately feel about the decision? What did the experience teach you both?

WEEK 4: WHITE WATER
Chapter 8: Gratitude Is a Choice

1. What are some of the things you are most grateful for in your own life? How might you say thank you to God and others for those things today?

2. Do you feel your children understand the plight of others around the world who have so much less than families do in the West? What are some ways your family can bless

others through serving and giving together? (For ideas
to get you started, see Appendix C in this book or visit
www.raisinggratefulkids.com.) How could teaching your
children about helping others simultaneously cultivate a
grateful spirit?

Chapter 9: Where the Rubber Meets the Road

1. Can you identify an area in your own home right now
   that needs some hard work and elbow grease? How
   might you work together as a family to accomplish it?
   In what parts could you invite a child to take charge
   and own a leadership role?

2. How would you score on the "marshmallow test?" What
   about your kids? What does this reveal about each of you?

3. Why do you think working for a goal makes the earned
   reward even more special?

4. When do you see your family at its absolute best? What
   do you appreciate about your family in those moments?

5. Kristen believes we were all created to ask the question,
   What can I do that matters? After reading this book, how
   would you answer that question on behalf of yourself
   and your family?

Chapter 10: Dear Parents

1. What kind of atmosphere do you want to create and
   cultivate in your home? What do you want your kids'
   memories of growing up to be? What qualities do you

want your children to have as adults, and what are you doing now to help them develop those?

2. "When you decide to push against a cultural norm," Kristen says, "there will be people in your life and community, even your church, who will question you." From where do you anticipate pushback in your quest to cultivate different values in your home? What will encourage you and help you to stand strong?

3. What do you see as the key differences between times when you *give in to your kids* vs. times when you *choose relationship over rules*?

4. Kristen shares her dream for a grateful family in these words:

> I would love for my kids to say one day they
> are grateful for their lives because their dad and
> I were grateful for ours. I want them to have
> memories of me thanking God for all He's done.
> I want them to catch me writing thank-you
> notes and being generous with my time and
> money because God has been generous with me.
> But most of all, I want my children to know
> that we wanted them to resist the current of
> our culture and choose a lifestyle of gratitude
> because we love them deeply and completely.

As you finish reading this book, what are your biggest hopes and prayers for your own? How has the countercultural message of *Raising Grateful Kids in an Entitled World* inspired, challenged, or emboldened you for the journey?

NOTES

INTRODUCTION

1. Dan Kindlon, *Too Much of a Good Thing* (New York: Miramax, 2001), xi.
2. Ibid.
3. *Merriam-Webster OnLine*, s.v. "entitlement," http://www.merriam-webster .com/dictionary/entitlement.

CHAPTER 1: WANTS VS. NEEDS

1. James Truslow Adams, *The Epic of America* (Boston: Little, Brown, and Company, 1931), 214–215.
2. *Merriam-Webster OnLine*, s.v. "American dream," http://www.merriam -webster.com/dictionary/american%20dream.
3. Heather Levin, "5 Reasons You Should Buy a Small House," *US News*, October 4, 2011, http://money.usnews.com/money/blogs/my-money /2011/10/04/5-reasons-you-should-buy-a-small-house; and Mary Ellen Podmolik, "Average Home Size Sets New Record, *Chicago Tribune*, June 2, 2014, http://articles.chicagotribune.com/2014-06-02/business /chi-average-home-size-sets-new-record-20140603_1_home-size-home -builders-new-record.
4. Howard R. Gold, "Price Tag for the American Dream: $130K a Year," *USA Today*, July 4, 2014, http://www.usatoday.com/story/money/personal finance/2014/07/04/american-dream/11122015/.
5. *The Charters of Freedom*, "The Declaration of Independence: A Transcription," http://www.archives.gov/exhibits/charters/declaration_transcript.html.
6. Joshua Becker, "The American Dream Does Not Cost $130,000/Year," *Becoming Minimalist*, http://www.becomingminimalist.com/american -dream/.

7. Gary Chapman and Arlene Pellicane, *Growing Up Social* (Chicago: Northfield, 2014), 55.
8. Richard and Linda Eyre, *The Entitlement Trap* (New York: Penguin, 2011), 2, italics in original.

CHAPTER 2: TIMES HAVE CERTAINLY CHANGED
1. "Opie and the Spoiled Kid" was season 3, episode 21; the third season first aired in 1962–1963. You can see this episode online by googling the title.
2. This was posted on August 24, 2014 at http://www.scarymommy.com /back-to-school-the-70s-vs-today#sthash.H6NqMCQD.dpuf, then picked up by http://www.huffingtonpost.com/victoria-fedden/back-to-school-the -70s-vs-today_b_5716891.html. Please note that there is sensitive language on the website and in the complete version of the post that may be offensive to readers.
3. Josh McDowell, *Right from Wrong* (Dallas: Word Publishing, 1994), 18.
4. "Barna Survey Examines Changes in Worldview among Christians over the Past 13 Years," BarnaGroup, March 6, 2009, https://www.barna.org/barna -update/21-transformation/252-barna-survey-examines%20-changes-in -worldview-among-christians-over-the-past-13-years#.VZFf9GrbJAE.
5. McDowell, *Right from Wrong*, 97.
6. David Platt, *Counter Culture* (Carol Stream, IL: Tyndale House Publishers, 2015), 1, italics in original.
7. Proverbs 22:6, NKJV
8. Gary D. Pratico and Miles V. Van Pelt, *Basics of Biblical Hebrew Grammar* (Grand Rapids: Zondervan, 2007), 162.
9. Douglas K. Stuart, "'The Cool of the Day' (Gen. 3:8) and 'The Way He Should Go' (Prov. 22:6)," *Bibliotheca Sacra* 171, no. 683 (July–September 2014), 271, italics in original.
10. Pratico and Van Pelt, *Basics of Biblical Hebrew Grammar*, 162.

CHAPTER 3: SEVEN WAYS WE PARENTS MISS THE BOAT (AND HOW TO GET ON BOARD)
1. Jen Wilkin, "'Stuff,' Satisfaction, and the Suburban Child," *The Beginning of Wisdom* (blog), November 24, 2010, http://jenwilkin.blogspot.com /2010/11/stuff-satisfaction-and-suburban-child.html.
2. Dan Kindlon, *Too Much of a Good Thing* (New York: Miramax, 2001), 20.
3. Ibid., 23.
4. Elizabeth W. Dunn and Michael Norton, "Don't Indulge. Be Happy.," *New York Times*, July 7, 2012, http://www.nytimes.com/2012/07/08 /opinion/sunday/dont-indulge-be-happy.html?_r=2&emc=eta1.
5. Robert Glatter, "How Much Money Do You Really Need to Be Happy?," *Forbes*, July 27, 2012, http://www.forbes.com/sites/robert glatter/2012/07/27/how-much-money-do-you-need-to-be-happy-2/.

6. Lori Gottlieb, "How to Land Your Kid in Therapy," *The Atlantic*, July /August 2011. Please note that there is sensitive language in this article that may be offensive to readers.
7. Ibid.
8. Quoted in Lori Gottlieb, "How to Land Your Kid in Therapy."
9. Jen Wilkin, "'Stuff,' Satisfaction, and the Suburban Child."
10. Ibid.

CHAPTER 4: THE SELFIE SOCIETY

1. Steve Baskin, "The Gift of Failure," *Psychology Today* blog post, December 31, 2011, http://www.psychologytoday.com/blog/smores -and-more/201112/the-gift-failure.
2. *Oxford Dictionaries* online, s.v. "special," http://www.oxforddictionaries .com/us/definition/american_english/special.
3. "Oxford Dictionaries Word of the Year 2013," *Oxford Dictionaries*, OxfordWord blog, November 19, 2013, http://blog.oxforddictionaries .com/press-releases/oxford-dictionaries-word-of-the-year-2013/.
4. "'Twerking' and 'Selfie' Added to Oxford Dictionary," *BBC News*, August 28, 2013, http://www.bbc.com/news/entertainment-arts-23861702.
5. Shephali Bhatt, "Selfie Grows from a Dictionary Entry to a Global Phenomenon," *Economic Times*, August 27, 2014, http://articles.economic times.indiatimes.com/2014-08-27/news/53284996_1_mtv-india-shopping -mall-philips.
6. Chris Welch, "'Star Wars' Launches Official Instagram Account with Darth Vader Selfie," *The Verge*, December 2, 2013, http://www.theverge.com/2013 /12/2/5167648/star-wars-launches-instagram-account-with-darth-vader -selfie.
7. Leah Bourne, "New Infographic Shows That Over a Million Selfies Are Taken Every Day," *StyleCaster*, March 20, 2014, http://stylecaster.com /selfies-infographic/#ixzz3FfmLiEEF.
8. "'Duck face' . . . is a pejorative term for a facial expression made by pressing one's lips together into the shape of a duck's bill" per "Duck Face," *Know Your Meme*, http://knowyourmeme.com/memes/duck-face.
9. Kate Knibbs, "Selfies Are Now the Most Popular Genre of Photo," *Digital Trends*, June 20, 2013, http://www.digitaltrends.com/social-media/ selfies-are-now-the-most-popular-genre-of-picture-and-in-related-news -everyones-the-worst/#ixzz3FfoTqWIx.
10. Also known as Millennials, these are people born in the 1980s and 1990s. See *Merriam-Webster OnLine*, s.v. "Generation Y," http://www.merriam -webster.com/dictionary/generation%20y.
11. "As College Graduates Hit the Workforce, So Do More Entitlement-Minded Workers," University of New Hampshire Media Relations, May 17, 2010, http://www.unh.edu/news/cj_nr/2010/may/lw17gen-y.cfm.

12. "'Gen Y' Interns: 7 Reasons Why They Are Good Hires," Internships.com Employer Resources, http://www.internships.com/employer/resources/recruit/whygen-y.

13. Steve Baskin, "The Gift of Failure."

14. James Sheridan, "Marriage Advice: 'Couple-Centered' Marriages the Healthiest for Parents and Children," *News-Sentinel,* March 14, 2012, http://www.news-sentinel.com/apps/pbcs.dll/article?AID=/20120314/LIVING/303149999/1054.

15. David McCullough, Wellesley High School Commencement Address delivered June 1, 2012, AmericanRhetoric.com, http://www.americanrhetoric.com/speeches/PDFFiles/David%20McCullough%20-%20Wellesley%20HS%20Commencement.pdf.

16. Dave Stone, *How to Raise Selfless Kids in a Self-Centered World* (Nashville: Thomas Nelson, 2012), 11.

17. Ibid., 34, 44, italics in original.

CHAPTER 5: MAKING SMART CHOICES ABOUT TECHNOLOGY

1. Eric Rice et al., "Sexting and Sexual Behavior among Middle School Students," *Pediatrics,* April 17, 2014, http://pediatrics.aappublications.org/content/early/2014/06/25/peds.2013-2991.

2. Doug Gross, "Social Networks and Kids: How Young Is Too Young?" *CNN,* November 3, 2009, http://www.cnn.com/2009/TECH/11/02/kids.social.networks/.

3. Chris Morris, "Porn Industry Feeling Upbeat about 2014," *NBC News,* January 14, 2014, http://www.nbcnews.com/business/business-news/porn-industry-feeling-upbeat-about-2014-n9076.

4. John Bingham, "Sexting and Porn Part of Everyday Life for Teenagers," *The Telegraph,* August 20, 2014, http://www.telegraph.co.uk/women/sex/better-sex-education/11043935/Sexting-and-porn-part-of-everyday-life-for-teenagers.html.

5. "87 Percent of Teens Sleep with Their Cell Phones and Other Alarming Statistics," *PE HUB,* April 20, 2010, https://www.pehub.com/2010/04/87-percent-of-teens-sleep-with-their-cell-phones-and-other-alarming-statistics/.

6. "Christian Parents Are Not Comfortable with Media but Buy Them for Their Kids Anyway," BarnaGroup, November 19, 2007, https://www.barna.org/barna-update/family-kids/90-christian-parents-are-not-comfortable-with-media-but-buy-them-for-their-kids-anyway#.VZVo7mrbJAE.

7. For our backstory, see Kristen Welch, *Rhinestone Jesus* (Carol Stream, IL: Tyndale House Publishers, 2014).

8. "Policy Statement: Media Use by Children Younger than 2 Years," American Academy of Pediatrics, *Pediatrics* 128, no. 5 (November 2011), http://pediatrics.aappublications.org/content/early/2011/10/12/peds.2011-1753.

CHAPTER 6: CULTIVATING OBEDIENCE

1. Sally Clarkson, "First Time Obedience, Really? Another View into the Process," *Own Your Life in 2015* (blog), September 6, 2012, http://sally clarkson.com/first-time-obedience-really-another-view-into-the-process/.

2. Sally Clarkson, "First Time Obedience, Really? Revisited and a Giveaway of Heartfelt Discipline!," *Own Your Life in 2015* (blog), April 9, 2013, http://sallyclarkson.com/first-time-obedience-really/.

3. Tedd Tripp, *Shepherding a Child's Heart* (Wapwallopen, PA: Shepherd Press, 1995), 204.

4. Ashley Merryman, "Losing Is Good for You," *New York Times*, September 24, 2013, http://www.nytimes.com/2013/09/25/opinion/losing-is-good -for-you.html?_r=1.

5. Ibid.

6. Ibid.

7. Ibid.

8. Dictionary.com, s.v. "adultescent" (see also "adultolescent"), http:// dictionary.reference.com/browse/adultescent.

9. "Bringing Up Adultolescents," *Newsweek*, March 24, 2002, http://www .newsweek.com/bringing-adultolescents-141705.

10. Ibid.

CHAPTER 7: LIVING OUT GOD'S LOVE IN YOUR HOME

1. William Farley, *Gospel-Powered Parenting* (Phillipsburg, NJ: P&R Publishing, 2009), Kindle version.

2. "Building a Christ-Centered Home," Focus on the Family (online forum), July 7, 2015, italics in original, http://family.custhelp.com/app/answers /detail/a_id/25919/~/what-does-it-mean-to-have-a-christ-centered -home%3F.

3. Alvin Reid, "6 Ways to Make Christ Central at Home," Gospel-Centered Discipleship (GCD), http://gcdiscipleship.com/6-ways-to-make-christ -central-at-home/.

4. Ibid.

5. Ibid.

6. Ibid.

7. "Building a Christ-Centered Home," Focus on the Family (online forum), italics in original.

8. The Jesse Tree is an Advent custom that tells the genealogy of Jesus, starting at Creation and continuing through the coming of the Messiah.

9. Ann Voskamp, *Unwrapping the Greatest Gift* (Carol Stream, IL: Tyndale House Publishers, 2014).

10. Ibid., 7.

11. Ibid., 8.

12. Tedd Tripp, *Shepherding a Child's Heart* (Wapwallopen, PA: Shepherd Press, 1995), 131–211.

13. Jay Younts, "Understanding the Difference between Influence and Authority," a blog on the Shepherd Press website, http://www.shepherd press.com/understanding-the-difference-between-influence-and-authority/.

14. Quoted in "Gospel-Powered Parenting: Avoiding a Child-Centered Home," *Generation Cedar* (blog), http://www.generationcedar.com/main/2010/10 /gospel-powered-parenting-avoiding-a-child-centered-hom.html.

15. Sally Lloyd-Jones, *The Jesus Storybook Bible* (Grand Rapids: Zondervan, 2007).

CHAPTER 8: GRATITUDE IS A CHOICE

1. Ben Stein, "Lessons in Gratitude, at the Basement Sink," *New York Times*, June 5, 2005, http://www.nytimes.com/2005/06/05/business/yourmoney /lessons-in-gratitude-at-the-basement-sink.html?_r=0.

2. Amit Amin, "The Science of Gratitude: More Benefits than Expected; 26 Studies and Counting," *Happier Human*, http://happierhuman.com /the-science-of-gratitude/.

3. Robert Emmons, *Thanks!: How the New Science of Gratitude Can Make You Happier* (New York: Houghton Mifflin, 2007), 7.

4. Ibid.

5. Robert Emmons, "What Gets in the Way of Gratitude?" *Greater Good*, November 12, 2013, http://greatergood.berkeley.edu/article/item/what _stops_gratitude.

6. Ibid.

7. Quoted by Yasmin Anwar, "Teaching Kids Gratitude Instead of Entitlement," *Berkeley News*, November 22, 2010, http://news.berkeley .edu/2010/11/22/gratitude/.

8. Emmons, *Thanks!*, 189.

9. Ibid., 203.

10. Jeremy Adam Smith, "Six Habits of Highly Grateful People," *Greater Good*, November 20, 2013, http://greatergood.berkeley.edu/article/item /six_habits_of_highly_grateful_people.

11. Ibid.

12. Robert Emmons, "How Gratitude Can Help You through Hard Times," *Greater Good*, May 13, 2013, http://greatergood.berkeley.edu/article/item /how_gratitude_can_help_you_through_hard_times.

13. Quoted in Jeremy Adam Smith, "Six Habits of Highly Grateful People."

14. You can read Christine Carter's full article, "Teenagers: Are Yours More Entitled than Grateful?" at *Greater Good, Raising Happiness* (blog), November 18, 2010, http://greatergood.berkeley.edu/raising_happiness /post/teenagers_are_yours_more_entitled_than_grateful/.

CHAPTER 9: WHERE THE RUBBER MEETS THE ROAD

1. Mary Hunt, *Raising Financially Confident Kids* (Grand Rapids: Revell, 2012).
2. *Wikipedia*, s.v. "delayed gratification," last modified May 13, 2015, https://en.wikipedia.org/wiki/Delayed_gratification.
3. "Delaying Gratification," American Psychological Association, https://www.apa.org/helpcenter/willpower-gratification.pdf.

CHAPTER 10: DEAR PARENTS

1. Alex and Brett Harris, *Do Hard Things: A Teenage Rebellion against Low Expectations* (Colorado Springs: Multnomah, 2008), 25.
2. David Platt, *Counter Culture* (Carol Stream, IL: Tyndale House Publishers, 2015), xiv.

ABOUT THE AUTHOR

KRISTEN WELCH is a Texas girl, born and raised in the South. It wasn't until she became a busy mother of three that she began to blog about her life on WeAreTHATFamily.com. Over the years, Kristen has grown a vast following of moms who identify with her real, often funny, and always inspiring writing.

In 2010, Kristen traveled with Compassion International to Kenya on a blogging trip to write about poverty in a huge slum. That experience turned her world upside down, and as a result, she and her family founded a nonprofit called Mercy House, which endeavors to empower and disciple impoverished women around the world. You can learn more about how this ministry started in Kristen's memoir, *Rhinestone Jesus*. She is also one of DaySpring's (in)Courage writers, a frequent speaker, and a regular columnist in *ParentLife* magazine.

Kristen's blog following continues to grow, and many of the readers financially support the work of Mercy House. When they aren't in Kenya, Kristen and her husband and their three children live in Texas, where they enjoy going to football games and flea markets and trying new restaurants.

TO READ MORE *about Kristen's family and* what *their biggest yes turned out to be, read* Rhinestone Jesus . . .

foreword by ANN VOSKAMP

rhinestone

JESUS

SAYING YES TO GOD
*when sparkly, safe faith
is no longer enough*

KRISTEN WELCH
— Author of *We Are THAT Family* blog —

ISBN 978-1-4143-8942-4

A JOURNEY FROM A SAFE, "GOOD-GIRL" FAITH to realizing that God was daring her and her family to a bolder, more authentic, more dangerous way of living. Don't settle for a shiny, ornamental faith—discover one that's messy, courageous, and more fulfilling than you ever imagined.

CP1051